entertaining

acknowledgments

I would like to thank: Anne Wilson, Catie Ziller, Mark Smith, Mark Newman and all the staff at Murdoch-Merehurst for the great opportunity and for their commitment to the book; Matt Handbury, head of a diverse and dynamic company, for allowing me to create this book; Jackie Frank for her commitment to Australian *marie claire* and my work there as food editor; Petrina for her commitment to perfection, for making the images so beautiful and for laughing at my jokes until the bitter end—cha cha cha; Michèle for her talents in design and for her endless patience; Rowena for whipping my words into style, for patience and for keeping me to a tight schedule, which is no mean feat; my partner Billy, who has now survived two books with me, for letting me yell at him, cry on his shoulder and generally be painful during the making of the book; Jody, a great friend and colleague who I simply couldn't be without, for always believing in me; Michaela for persisting with the recipe testing, for the long days of food preparation during photography and for being the model as well; Con and Nadine for being not only photographic assistants but stand-in models and suppliers of caffeine, and for staying with the program; Paula for racing all over the place to find the unfindable props I so often ask for; and my family for their support and understanding.

credits

The author would like to thank the following people and organisations for their generosity in supplying props and product for the book: Anticos Fruitworld; Demcos Seafood Providores; Simon Johnson Purveyor of Quality Foods; Georges Department Store, The Conran Shop; Country Road Homewares; Country Road Women's Clothing; Breville Appliances; Empire Homewares; Orrefors Kosta Boda; Hamish Clark Antiques; E.P. Manchester; Dinosaur Designs; Camargue; Orson & Blake Homewares; The Bay Tree; Tea Two; Ventura Designs for Alessi; Grinders Coffee; Pam Harvey (Grant's Mum) for knitting 'Fluffy' the tea cosy; Ellie Ellis for allowing me to use her family's kitchen heirlooms as props; Rachel Blackmore for linen lining the baskets; Peter Tinslay for the beautiful old books; Chris for the bamboo steamers from Hong Kong.

This edition published in the United States and Canada by Whitecap Books.
First published by Murdoch Books®, a division of Murdoch Magazines Pty Ltd, 45 Jones Street, Ultimo NSW 2007.

Recipes and Styling: Donna Hay
Photographer: Petrina Tinslay
Designer: Michèle Lichtenberger
Editor: Rowena Lennox

CEO & Publisher: Anne Wilson; Associate Publisher/Publishing Director: Catie Ziller; International Sales Director: Mark Newman

A catalogue record for this book is available from the National Library of Australia
ISBN 0 86411 806 6

Text © Donna Hay 1998. Design and photography © Murdoch Books® 1998.
Printed by Toppan Printing (S) Pte. Ltd, Singapore. First printed 1998.
PRINTED IN SINGAPORE.

Distributed in Canada by Whitecap Books (Vancouver) Ltd, 351 Lynn Avenue, North Vancouver, BC V7J 2C4,
Telephone (604) 980 9852, Facsimile (604) 980 8197 or Whitecap Books (Ontario) Ltd, 47 Coldwater Road, North York, ON,
M3B 1Y8, Telephone (416) 444 3442, Facsimile (416) 444 6630
Distributed in the USA by Graphic Arts Centre Publishing, PO Box 10306, Portland, OR 97296-0306, USA
Telephone (503) 226 2402, Facsimile 1 503 294 9900

entertaining

donna hay

photography by
petrina tinslay

WHITECAP
BOOKS

contents

introduction

Entertaining is about sharing food, wine, good conversation and a laugh or two with friends. Great memories are often made around a table of delicious food and drinks.

The recipes in this book range from simple yet stylish weeknight dinner solutions to food for the most formal dining experience. You'll find information about planning menus and selecting wines, as well as all the basics you'll need for any culinary occasion. Continuing in *the new cook* style, *entertaining* offers inspirational recipes with innovative serving ideas and refreshing liquid suggestions. There are menu ideas for each chapter, but please feel free to create your own menus from any of the chapters.

More information about ingredients and cooking terms marked with a star* can be found in the glossary. Turn to the glossary for basic recipes, which are also marked in the text with a star*.

menus

Putting together a menu is easy. If you follow a few simple guides, you can choose foods that will complement each other and flow to form a complete dining experience.
Avoid doubling up on flavours, cream-based recipes and ingredients. For example, if you are serving a Thai chicken salad as a starter, don't serve a spice-crusted grilled chicken breast as a main meal. Also, avoid doubling up on some cooking methods such as deep frying. It is fine to have 1 deep-fried course but serving 2 courses of deep-fried food would be too heavy.

planning a menu

Continuity is important in a menu. If you were to serve an Asian meal flavoured with chillies, lime and fresh Asian herbs, a chocolate dessert would not be in continuity with the menu. You could try, for example, a lime and green apple sorbet or grilled mangoes instead.

As a guide, serve lighter foods first. By lighter foods, I don't mean not well-flavoured foods, but foods that are not too heavy and complex. A very complex and lavish starter followed by a similar style of main meal may be a little heavy on the stomach. It's better to serve a simply flavoured starter followed by a more complex main meal. The flavours need to build on each other and develop through the menu. If you are aware that the people you are dining with enjoy very rich foods, you could always bend this guideline.

The food you choose and the style in which you decide to present it should be in keeping with the style of dining you wish to have. For example, an Asian banquet of delicately steamed morsels to be shared usually results in a less formal occasion than a 3–4 course meal. To make an occasion more informal, have a table where food is set out for the guests to help themselves. Alternatively, have large platters and bowls at the table where you are sitting, so people can pick and choose what and how much they would like to eat.

serving success

A few little serving tips can help ensure the success of your dining experience.

To keep hot foods hot, warm the plates. If you are serving ice cream or sorbet in summer, it might be a good idea to chill the bowls or plates before serving.

Remember to change wine glasses when you serve a different wine. The residues of the previous wine could ruin the flavour of the new one.

If the occasion is formal and you have definite ideas on where you would like people to sit, place name cards on the table instead of ushering people around the table.

Serve drinks and something for your guests to nibble with their drinks as soon as they arrive. This will help them relax and feel comfortable.

Whatever drinks you are serving, place water glasses and water on the table.

If you are serving seafood with shells, have bowls on the table for discarding the unwanted bits and have finger bowls and warm towels so your guests can clean their hands.

timing is everything

Shop for dry goods and foods that will keep at least the day before your planned event. Pick up vegetables, meat and seafood on the day.

When planning your menu, choose some dishes that you can make ahead of time. Making the dessert or part of the starter or main meal beforehand will help the meal go smoothly and will ensure that you have time to enjoy yourself.

Remember to place wine, water and other drinks in the refrigerator or on ice well ahead of time.

Set the table with cutlery, napkins, underplates, glasses, serving ware, salt and pepper, condiments and anything else it requires before your guests arrive. With cutlery, start with the first course on the outside and work your way in. Bread plates should be on the left side of the setting, and wine glasses on the top right.

Remember to allow time to shower and dress before your guests are at the door.

wines

food and wine

When choosing wine to accompany your food, be aware that many different flavour levels are described by a simple word such as salad. A salad might be delicately flavoured greens and chervil with a light dressing and a soft quail egg, or it might be a robust combination of roast fennel slices, soft oven-roasted tomatoes, marinated olives and pan-fried haloumi cheese with a rich balsamic dressing. The wines you would select for these salads would be quite different. Use the following general recommendations as a guide only. Map out your food and wine choices together. Serve the wine before the food so your guests can taste it before adding the flavours of the food to their palates. There are no hard and fast rules about choosing wine. Try out some different combinations and remember, just because you had 1 bottle of sauvignon blanc that didn't excite the senses, the other 20 bottles of sauvignon blanc at the wine merchant's aren't all going to taste the same. Choosing wine is a personal thing—be adventurous!

whites

SEMILLON

Varies in colour according to the time the grape was picked and the age of the wine. Semillon ends up in bottles as 2 different wines. Ripe-picked grapes, with grassy, citrus flavours, make a young wine that fills the mouth with fresh flavours, usually ready to drink a year or 2 after harvest. Young semillon is also blended with sauvignon blanc and chardonnay. Early-picked semillon grapes, a little on the green side, start with a fairly bland taste but, with a good age, the wine takes on a honey and vanilla nose and has a rich and nutty flavour. General recommendations: fish, poultry, pork, rabbit, vegetables and salads.

SAUVIGNON BLANC

A crisp, dry wine, pale straw in colour, that has a variety of flavours from fresh-cut grass to asparagus and tropical fruits. A good sauvignon blanc should be fresh and almost cool tasting with lively flavours that awaken the mouth. General recommendations: salads, vegetables, Asian foods (for example, Thai, Vietnamese, Chinese and Malaysian) and smoked salmon.

CHARDONNAY

A broad, full-bodied wine, which has a range of melon and peach flavours when young, and buttery, fig and honey flavours with a bit of age. Chardonnay is often aged in wood or oak. This has sometimes been overdone, giving rise to the unwooded chardonnay, which had less obvious flavours. General recommendations: salads, vegetables, white meats and full-flavoured seafood.

RIESLING

A crisp and clean wine with a lemon and lime acidic taste that leaves the mouth fresh with a well-balanced fruitiness. This dry wine has a greenish tinge when young, and a floral and citrus aroma. If the grapes are cut late from the vine or infected with the botrytis strain, riesling makes a wonderful sweet dessert wine. General recommendations: seafood, Thai and Chinese foods, spicy foods and salads.

CHENIN BLANC

With a light citrus taste, this simple wine exhibits a dry palate, which is soft and full. Chenin blanc is a drink-now style of wine, perfect with a simple seafood meal. General recommendations: all seafood and mildly spiced foods.

VERDELHO

This wine has a very sleek texture. Flowery, citrus and fruit tastes make a dry wine with good body. General recommendations: pasta dishes, cream sauces, fish and fried foods.

SPARKLING

A great way to start a meal, bubbly white refreshes the mouth and plays on the tongue. Most sparkling wines are ready to drink when they are released, although some vintage wines need to be cellared so their tastes develop. General recommendations: pre-dinner morsels, seafood and celebrations.

glasses

Drink wine from glasses that are made for drinking wine. It really will make a difference when you are drinking quality wine. Be sure that the glasses you choose slope inwards towards the top rim so all the wonderful aromas of the wine head in the direction of your nose.

tasting wine

To start, pour a small amount of wine into a glass. Look at the colour of the wine as it will often tell you a lot, for example, a green tint to a sauvigon blanc will indicate a fresh and perhaps grassy taste. If it is in good condition, the wine should be crystal clear and bright.

Next, swirl the wine around the glass, hold it up to your nose and have a good sniff—just like testing a fine perfume. Learn to recognise the aromas of different wine, for example, a lemony, grassy young sauvignon blanc contrasted with the peppery, berry and wooded aromas of a good shriaz.

Now, take a very small sip of the wine and allow it to move around your mouth, making sure it covers all the tastebuds on your tongue. While the wine is in your mouth, take a short, small in-breath and allow the aromas of the wine to fill your mouth all the way to the back of your throat. You will not only be tasting the wine's characteristics but you will also feel its texture, for example, the viscosity and thick smoothness of a sticky dessert wine or the velvety softness of a pinot noir.

After all this hard work and assessment, swallow.

reds

PINOT NOIR

A smooth, light red wine that has a range of flavours from berry fruits and cherry to spice and earthiness. Pinot noir is a wine with intense flavour and a clean, fresh and velvety soft mouth feel. General recommendations: full-flavoured fish such as tuna and Atlantic salmon, duck and game meats, some spicy foods, pâté, terrines and pasta dishes.

CABERNET SAUVIGNON

With blackcurrant and faint new-oak or cedarwood smells, cabernet sauvignon is a great robust and flexible wine with medium-to-full body, a lingering full finish, and loads of tannin and acidity. General recommendations: beef, lamb and some game meats.

MERLOT

Merlot is most commonly found blended with cabernet sauvignon. It is a soft low-acid and low-tannin wine but still has a full, rich, round flavour. When it isn't blended, merlot is extremely round and mellow. General recommendations: red meats, Italian food and cheeses.

SHIRAZ

A dark and full-flavoured wine, exhibiting berry and spice flavours that are sometimes even peppery and earthy, with a soft oak finish. Shiraz has a generous flavour with softer tannin and acid than cabernet sauvignon, making these 2 perfect blending partners. General recommendations: beef, veal, game meats, mature cheeses and smoked foods.

GRENACHE

A wine that is often blended with a shiraz or mourvèdre (mataro) because of its full-spice and ripe-fruit flavours. Once blended, grenache improves to become a rich, spicy wine. General recommendations: Middle Eastern food, garlic-rich foods and spiced meats.

coffee & cake

basics

Coffee is the seed from a type of evergreen cherry tree that grows in a narrow subtropical belt around the world. At first, small clusters of jasmine-like flowers appear on the tree, then small green cherries. The cherries take 6–9 months to ripen, changing from green to yellow to red until they become dark and almost black. The coffee cherries are picked by hand as they ripen at different times. Each coffee cherry contains 2 green coffee beans and it takes 4000 coffee beans to produce 500g (1 lb) of roasted coffee.

processing

After they are picked, the coffee cherries are processed to remove the cherry flesh so that only the beans remain. This is done either by drying the cherries and removing the fruit by husking, or by soaking them. The green beans are then sorted and graded by hand and transported all around the world for roasting.

roasting

Roasting caramelises the sugars and carbohydrates in the coffee bean, creating coffee oil, which is where coffee's flavour and aroma come from. A lightly roasted bean, the colour of cinnamon to light chocolate, is used for espresso, as lighter roasts produce a sharper and more acidic taste than darker roasts. The darker the roast, the less caffeine and acidity.

blending

Coffee beans differ in flavour according to the coffee tree's growing conditions and location. A full-flavoured and balanced coffee is produced by blending. Beans of the same type grown in different places are often blended for the perfect coffee. Many espresso coffees contain 3–7 different beans to create the necessary complexity.

grind guide

Percolator: coarse
Electric drip or French press (plunger): medium
Espresso and filter-cone drip: very fine

10 steps to better coffee

- Use fresh coffee beans. Store beans at a cool room temperature away from strong food odours. Unless you need to store beans for a prolonged period of time, they should not be frozen, as freezing affects the taste of the coffee.
- Air and moisture are the enemies of coffee, so keep your coffee in a well-sealed container.
- Coffee is at its best when consumed within 24–72 hours after roasting. The flavour diminishes substantially after 7–10 days. Old coffee beans look oily.
- Be sure your coffee is ground to fit your purpose and taste.
- For a great coffee, grind your beans just before making coffee.
- If you do not purchase quality coffee, how can you expect a good cup of coffee?
- Use the right amount of coffee—a good general guide is 2 level tablespoons of coffee per cup.
- Be sure that your coffee-making equipment (plungers, espresso machines and so on) is clean and free from any ground coffee or coffee oils.
- Warm your cup with boiling water before pouring coffee.
- Before serving, give the cup of coffee a stir to ensure that you distribute the heavier coffee oils, and therefore stronger flavours, throughout the cup.

percolator

coffee beans

french press (plunger)

espresso machine

ground coffee

coconut and golden syrup wafers

chocolate shortbread sandwiches

coconut and golden syrup wafers

125g (4 oz) butter, chopped
1 cup caster (superfine) sugar
1/2 cup (4 fl oz) golden syrup
1 1/3 cups plain (all-purpose) flour
1 cup desiccated coconut
2 egg whites

Place butter and sugar in the bowl of an eletric mixer and beat until creamy. Add golden syrup to mixer and beat until combined. Stir flour, coconut and egg whites into mixture and refrigerate for 10 minutes.
Line baking trays with non-stick baking paper. Place tablespoons of mixture on lined trays and spread with a palette knife into rough 5cm (2 inch) circles. (Wafers will spread, so leave space between them.) Bake wafers in a preheated 180°C (350°F) oven for 8–10 minutes or until they are a light golden colour. Cool wafers on a wire rack. Serve with a macchiato. Makes 30.

chocolate shortbread sandwiches

125g (4 oz) butter
2/3 cup icing (confectioners) sugar
3/4 cup plain (all-purpose) flour
1/4 cup rice flour
1/3 cup cocoa powder
filling
125g (4 oz) dark chocolate
1/4 cup (2 fl oz) cream

Place butter and icing (confectioners) sugar in the bowl of an electric mixer, and beat until light and creamy.
Add flour, rice flour and cocoa powder, and mix until a smooth dough forms.
Roll out dough between sheets of non-stick baking paper until it is 2mm (1/8 inch) thick. Cut dough into 6cm (2 1/2 inch) circles and place them on a baking tray lined with non-stick baking paper.
Bake dough circles in a preheated 160°C (315°F) oven for 15 minutes or until biscuits are firm to touch. Cool biscuits on wire racks.
To make filling, place chocolate and cream in a saucepan over low heat and stir until smooth. Refrigerate mixture until it is firm.
To serve, sandwich 2 biscuits together with a spoonful of chocolate filling. Makes 12.

parchment blueberry and passionfruit muffins

parchment paper and string
1 3/4 cups plain (all-purpose) flour, sifted
1 1/2 teaspoons baking powder
1 cup caster (superfine) sugar
1 teaspoon ground cinnamon
1 cup sour cream
60g (2 oz) soft butter
2 teaspoons grated lemon rind
1 egg
1/3 cup (2 3/4 fl oz) passionfruit pulp
1 cup blueberries

Roll small lengths of parchment paper into 8 cylinders 8cm (3 inches) high and 6cm (2 1/2 inches) wide, and secure with string. Place parchment cylinders in 1/2-cup capacity ramekins to fit on a lined baking tray.
Place flour, baking powder, sugar and cinnamon in a bowl and mix to combine. Place sour cream, butter, lemon rind, egg and passionfruit in a separate bowl and mix to combine.
Add sour cream mixture to dry ingredients and mix until just combined. Sprinkle blueberries over mixture and spoon into parchment cylinders until they are just over three-quarters full. Bake muffins in a preheated 180°C (350°F) oven for 35–40 minutes or until they are cooked when tested with a skewer. Serve warm with caffè lattes for breakfast or morning snacks. Makes 8.

espresso granita

3 cups (24 fl oz) hot water
1 cup sugar
2 cups (16 fl oz) prepared strong coffee

Place water, sugar and coffee in a pan over low heat and stir until sugar has dissolved. Bring mixture to the boil and simmer for 3 minutes.
Pour mixture into a metal container and freeze for 3 hours. Mash with a fork and return to freezer for another 3 hours. Serve as a summer breakfast or as a hot afternoon pick-me-up. Serves 6.

parchment blueberry and passionfruit muffins

espresso syrup cakes

155g (5 oz) butter
2/3 cup caster (superfine) sugar
1 teaspoon vanilla essence
1 egg
1 1/2 cups self-raising (self-rising) flour
2 tablespoons prepared espresso
2 tablespoons milk
espresso syrup
1 cup (8 fl oz) prepared strong espresso
1/3 cup sugar
1–2 tablespoons coffee liqueur

Place butter and sugar in a bowl, and beat until light and creamy. Add vanilla and egg, and beat well. Fold sifted flour into butter mixture with espresso and milk.
Spoon mixture into eight 8cm (3 inch) round cake tins or 1/2-cup capacity muffin pans and bake in a preheated 180°C (350°F) oven for 20 minutes or until cakes are cooked when tested with a skewer.
To make syrup, place espresso, sugar and liqueur in a saucepan over low heat and stir until sugar has dissolved. Allow syrup to simmer for 4–6 minutes or until it has thickened. To serve, invert warm cakes onto serving plates and top with espresso syrup and thick cream. Makes 12.

espresso shots

4 tablespoons coffee beans
3/4 cup (6 fl oz) cream
70g (2 1/4 oz) dark chocolate
3 tablespoons coffee or chocolate liqueur

Place coffee beans and cream in a saucepan over low heat and simmer for 4–5 minutes, allow to stand for 20 minutes, then strain. Return cream to pan, add chocolate and stir until smooth. Stir liqueur through cream. Pour mixture into shot glasses and refrigerate until set. Serve as a summer-afternoon cooler or as a smooth after-dinner shot. Serves 6.

portuguese custard tarts

1 quantity (350g or 12 oz) sweet flaky pastry* or prepared
    puff pastry
filling
1/3 cup sugar
1/3 cup (2 3/4 fl oz) water
2 cups (16 fl oz) milk
2 tablespoons cornflour (cornstarch)
2 egg yolks
1 teaspoon vanilla essence

Roll out pastry on a lightly floured surface until it is 3mm (1/8 inch) thick. Cut pastry into 10cm (4 inch) circles and place in patty tins so pastry comes up the side of the tin. To make filling, place sugar and water in a saucepan over low heat and stir until sugar has dissolved. Simmer syrup for 1 minute. Mix a little of the milk with the cornflour (cornstarch) to make a smooth paste. Whisk together remaining milk, cornflour (cornstarch) paste, sugar syrup, egg yolks and vanilla, and place in a saucepan over low heat. Stir until mixture thickens, then cool and cover surface of custard with plastic wrap.
Spoon filling into pastry shells. Bake in a preheated 200°C (400°F) oven for 20 minutes or until custard is golden and firm. Makes 8.

frozen caffè latte

500ml (16 fl oz) milk
1/3 cup (2 3/4 fl oz) prepared strong espresso, chilled
6 ice cubes

Place milk in the freezer for 3 hours or until it is frozen. Place milk, coffee and ice in a blender and blend until smooth. Pour latte into chilled glasses and serve immediately. Serves 2.

après café

6 tablespoons coarse-ground coffee
1 cinnamon stick
100g (3 1/2 oz) dark chocolate
4 1/2 cups (36 fl oz) milk

Place coffee, cinnamon, chocolate and milk in a saucepan and stir over medium heat until milk starts to boil. Pour mixture through a fine strainer and serve in warmed cups or glasses. Serve on a cold afternoon. Serves 4.

portuguese custard tart

brioche with chocolate centres

espresso granita   espresso shots

frozen caffè latte

après cafè

little nectarine cake

little nectarine cakes

125g (4 oz) butter, chopped
1 cup sugar
1 teaspoon vanilla essence
2 eggs
1⅓ cups plain (all-purpose) flour, sifted
1½ teaspoons baking powder
1 cup sour cream
⅓ cup ground almonds
3–4 nectarines, sliced
1 tablespoon demerara sugar

Place butter, sugar and vanilla in the bowl of an electric mixer, and beat until light and creamy. Add eggs, one at a time, and beat well. Sift flour and baking powder over butter mixture and fold through with sour cream and almonds. Spoon mixture into 8 lined 8½cm (3 inch) small round cake tins or large muffin tins. Top with nectarine slices and sprinkle with demerara sugar. Bake in a preheated 180°C (350°F) oven for 20–25 minutes or until cooked when tested with a skewer. Remove cakes from tins and serve warm with coffee. Makes 8.

brioche with chocolate centres

2 cups plain (all-purpose) flour
1½ teaspoons active dry yeast
½ cup (4 fl oz) warm milk
1 teaspoon vanilla essence
3 tablespoons sugar
2 egg yolks
125g (4 oz) butter, softened and chopped
8 large chunks of dark chocolate about 15g (½ oz) each

Place flour and yeast in the bowl of an electric mixer fitted with a dough hook. Place warm milk, vanilla and sugar in a separate bowl and mix until combined. Add milk mixture and egg yolks to flour and beat on medium speed until dough is a smooth ball. Continue beating, adding butter, a little at a time, until it is all incorporated and well beaten. Alternatively, mix the flour mixture and the yeast mixture in a bowl until a soft dough forms. Transfer dough to a lightly floured surface and knead until smooth. Add butter, a few pieces at a time, and knead until combined. Cover dough and set aside for 1½–2 hours or until it has doubled in size. Knead dough on a lightly floured surface until it is soft and elastic, then divide it into 8 pieces. Flatten dough slightly in the palm of your hand. Place a piece of chocolate in the middle of dough and fold over excess dough to enclose. Place brioche in greased and floured dariole moulds* or brioche tins, cover and set aside for 1 hour or until it is well risen. Bake in a preheated 180°C (350°F) oven for 15–20 minutes or until brioche are golden brown. Serve warm with strong caffè lattes. Makes 8.

chocolate and peach panforte

rice paper
1 cup (8 fl oz) liquid glucose
3/4 cup sugar
2 cups blanched almonds, toasted and roughly chopped
1 1/2 cups chopped dried peaches
1 1/2 cups plain (all-purpose) flour, sifted
1/3 cup cocoa powder
1 teaspoon ground cinnamon
180g (6 oz) dark chocolate, melted

Line the base and sides of an 18 x 28cm (7 x 11 inch) slice tin with rice paper and set aside.
Place glucose and sugar in a saucepan and stir over low heat until sugar has dissolved. When sugar has dissolved bring syrup to the boil and simmer for 2 minutes or until it has thickened slightly.
Place almonds, peaches, flour, cocoa and cinnamon in a bowl. Add syrup and chocolate, and mix until combined.
Firmly press mixture into prepared tin and bake in a preheated 180°C (350°F) oven for 20 minutes or until panforte is spongy to touch. Cool panforte in tin before cutting and serving with coffee. Makes 20 squares.
Note: rice paper in this recipe is the white rectangular paper often found on the outside of nougat or sweets.

caramel melting moments

250g (8 oz) butter
2/3 cup brown sugar
2 cups plain (all-purpose) flour
filling
90g (3 oz) butter
200g (6 1/2 oz) brown sugar
2 tablespoons golden syrup
1/3 cup (2 3/4 fl oz) thickened cream

Place butter and sugar in the bowl of an electric mixer and beat until light and creamy. Add flour and mix until combined.
Place tablespoons of biscuit mixture on lined baking trays. Bake in a preheated 160°C (315°F) oven for 15 minutes or until golden, and allow to cool on a wire rack.
To make filling, place butter, sugar, golden syrup and cream in a saucepan over low heat and mix until smooth. Allow caramel to simmer for 5 minutes or until it has thickened slightly.
Cool caramel in refrigerator until it is firm. Spread caramel over half the biscuits and sandwich them together with remaining biscuits. Serve with short black coffee. Makes 30.

chocolate and peach panforte

caramel melting moments

espresso syrup cakes

menu ideas

breakfast for 2

parchment blueberry and passionfruit muffins
espresso granita

FOOD PREP
To be organised for an early morning start, prepare
parchment paper cylinders and measure ingredients the night
before, then mix ingredients together and bake the muffins in
the morning.

LIQUID SUGGESTIONS
Ice-cold sparkling spring water with a wedge of lime and a
few mint leaves usually wakes the system. Try freezing
chopped fruit the night before, then, in the morning, putting it
in a blender with a splash of juice and blending until smooth.
For hot summer mornings, try serving espresso granita
instead of hot coffee. Freeze granita the night before.

coffee and a chat for 8

little nectarine cakes
chocolate shortbread sandwiches
après cafè

FOOD PREP
Bake chocolate shortbreads the day before and store them in
an airtight container. Fill shortbreads and sandwich them
together half an hour before serving. Little nectarine cakes
are best made the day of serving. If nectarines are
unavailable, use slices of fresh green apple or pear.

LIQUID SUGGESTIONS
If it's a mid-morning gossip, serve small bowls of après cafè
(x 2) or freshly squeezed ruby grapefruit juice over sparkling
mineral water.
For a lengthy afternoon debrief of what is really going on
around town, I suggest starting with a sweet sparkling wine
before coffee. For the brave, or for those who would rather sit
back and listen, a shot of grappa or pastis with a little iced
water may help your concentration.

post-dinner party for 6

chocolate and peach panforte
coconut and golden syrup wafers
espresso shots

FOOD PREP
Make chocolate and peach panforte up to 2 days ahead of
time and store it in an airtight container. Coconut and golden
syrup wafers can be made 1 day ahead and stored in an
airtight container once they are completely cooled.

LIQUID SUGGESTIONS
Smooth espresso shots (which need to be made ahead of
time) and a late-harvest or botrytis-affected riesling, well
chilled, will hit the spot. For a bit of adventure, try a well-aged
liqueur muscat or liqueur tokay.

coffee party for 12

espresso syrup cakes
caramel melting moments
little nectarine cakes
frozen caffè latte

FOOD PREP
Have a coffee party on those occasions when a lengthy
dinner is not required. Espresso syrup cakes can be made
ahead of time and warmed with their syrup. Bake little
nectarine cakes in small muffin tins for a shorter cooking time
and smaller cakes, so guests can sample all the goodies.
Bake biscuits for caramel melting moments the day before
and store in an airtight container. Spread biscuits with
caramel filling and sandwich together 1 hour before serving.

LIQUID SUGGESTIONS
If it is summer, serve frozen caffè lattes. For a large crowd,
make large plungers or French presses of coffee or have
somebody at the home espresso machine—whatever you do,
don't reheat coffee. For more serious liquids, a botrytis-
affected semillon or riesling, or a good aged port will work
well with the coffee and the sweet cakes.

asian steaming

2

basics

utensils

BAMBOO STEAMERS come in a variety of sizes. Buy 2 steamers with a tight-fitting lid, which fit on top of each other over a wok, or buy smaller steamers that fit over your saucepans. Soak new steamers in cold water for 2 hours before using them. Oil bases of steamers or line them with non-stick baking paper to prevent food from sticking.

STRAINER, with its long bamboo handle, is great for removing fried foods from the wok or for draining foods.

CHOPSTICKS are great for picking up yummy pieces of Asian foods, and noodles and sushi. They are also good for stirring ingredients and for placing across a wok to support a steamer.

SUSHI MAT is an essential inexpensive bamboo mat used to roll sushi rice and nori rolls.

wok, chan and brush

WOKS come in different varieties. Purchase a steel wok with a rounded base. Wash your wok well and season it before using by heating 2 tablespoons of oil over high heat until it is almost smoking. Brush oil over wok sides, cool wok and repeat this process 3 times or until the wok has a coating. Oil wok before storing so it does not rust.

WOK SPOON OR CHAN is great for tossing and lifting ingredients in a wok.

WOK BRUSH is a stiff bamboo brush used to clean your wok with minimal effort. It will not scratch the seasoned surface of the wok. After cleaning, place wok over high heat to dry.

sauces

SOY SAUCE ranges from light to dark and from sweet to salty. There are many different varieties. A good rule is: Chinese soy with Chinese food and Japanese soy with Japanese food. When using soy sauce, check the finished dish before serving. If the soy sauce you have used was too salty, add some shaved, crumbled palm sugar to reduce the saltiness.

OYSTER SAUCE is a fragrant, viscous sauce with oyster/seafood flavours. Buy good-quality oyster sauce that contains premium oyster extract.

FISH SAUCE is the clear amber liquid that drains from small fish that have been packed in wooden barrels with salt and fermented. Once you get past the aroma, the flavour becomes quite addictive.

PONZU is a great Japanese soy- and citrus-based sauce. Use it to marinate fish and seafood, and meats and chicken. It also makes a great dipping sauce and is available at Asian grocers.

asian greens

BOK CHOY has bright green leaves and pale green stems. The leaves and stems join to form a neat bunch. It is also available as baby bok choy.

CHOY SUM, with thin, even, crisp stems, bright green leaves and, often, yellow flowers, is great to steam or stir fry.

SNOW PEA SHOOTS are small, tender young shoots from the snow pea vine and have the same flavour as snow peas only a little milder. They are great in salads or stir fries.

GAI LARN, also known as Chinese broccoli, is easily recognisable because the stems resemble broccoli stems. It produces white flowers. Stems, leaves and flowers are edible, and leave a slightly bitter aftertaste.

essential ingredients

PALM SUGAR is made from the sap of a palm tree. Usually, the darker the sugar is, the better it is. Shave fine slices off the block with a knife or vegetable peeler. It is used to balance saltiness and to flavour sweets.

TAMARIND can be purchased as a soft, dried pulp from the tamarind bean. The stringy pulp and seeds need to be soaked in hot water and stirred with a fork or squeezed with your fingers to release the flavour.

MIRIN is cooking wine made from rice. Purchase pure (hon) mirin. japanese rice vinegar is a must for the sushi rice* lover. Steer away from the seasoned one, as it contains msg (monosodium glutamate).

CHILLI JAM is sold under many different names, including chilli paste with soy bean oil. It is a combination of chillies, fish sauce, shrimp paste, tamarind and shallots. Use it in cooking or as a dipping sauce.

SHAO HSING RICE WINE is Chinese cooking wine. Sweet sherry makes a good substitute.

asian herbs

VIETNAMESE MINT, with long, pointed leaves, has a distinctive spicy and slightly bitter, but refreshing, flavour.

KAFFIR LIME LEAVES look like two leaves joined together like a butterfly. They have a distinctive citrus smell and a wonderful flavour. Simmer them whole in dishes or shred them finely.

THAI BASIL has a sweeter flavour than Italian basil. It has purple stems and, often, purple veins running through its leaves.

sushi mat

bamboo steamers

wok, brush and chan

strainers

chopsticks

sauces

fish sauce and oyster sauce

palm sugar

tamarind pulp and chilli jam

shao hsing wine, rice vinegar and mirin

kaffir lime leaves

gai larn

choy sum

snow pea shoots

bok choy

thai basil

vietnamese mint

prawn and chilli pot-sticker dumplings

vinegared rice box with marinated sashimi

pork rice noodle rolls

spinach with sesame and soy

vinegared rice box with marinated sashimi

250g (8 oz) sashimi tuna, sliced
250g (8 oz) sashimi salmon, sliced
1 quantity sushi rice*
2 tablespoons Japanese rice vinegar
marinade
3 tablespoons soy sauce
1 tablespoon lemon juice
2 teaspoons black sesame seeds*
2 tablespoons mirin
1 teaspoon wasabi* paste
2 tablespoons bonito flakes*

To make marinade, place soy sauce, lemon juice, sesame seeds, mirin, wasabi and bonito flakes in a non-reactive bowl.* Allow marinade to stand for 2 hours, then strain. Place marinade in a large shallow dish. Place tuna and salmon in marinade. Marinade should only cover the base of the sashimi. Allow fish to marinate for 10 minutes. Place rice in 4 serving boxes and sprinkle with vinegar. Top rice with pieces of sashimi and serve marinade as a dipping sauce. Serve with pickled ginger, extra wasabi and soy sauce. Serves 6 as a starter, or 4 as a main meal.

prawn and chilli pot-sticker dumplings

500g (1 lb) green (raw) prawn meat, finely chopped
2 shallots, chopped
1 tablespoon shredded galangal* or ginger
1 tablespoon chopped coriander leaves
1 tablespoon chilli jam
2 tablespoons Chinese cooking (shao hsing) wine
1 tablespoon soy sauce
30 round wonton wrappers
1 tablespoon cornflour (cornstarch)
2 tablespoons water
1 tablespoon oil
1 cup (8 fl oz) vegetable* or fish stock*

Combine prawns, shallots, galangal, coriander, chilli jam, wine and soy sauce in a bowl. Place 1 tablespoon of mixture onto each wonton wrapper. Mix cornflour (cornstarch) and water to form a smooth paste and brush edges of wonton wrapper with paste. Fold wrapper in half, gather up edges like a fan and squeeze with fingertips to enclose filling.
Heat oil in a frypan over high heat. Add dumplings and fry bases until they are golden. Add stock and cover frypan. Allow dumplings to steam in stock for 3–4 minutes or until tender. Remove lid and allow stock to evaporate. Ensure bases of dumplings are crisp. Remove dumplings from pan and serve immediately with extra chilli jam. Makes 30.

pork rice noodle rolls

300g (10 oz) fresh plain rice noodle rolls or flat rice noodle
filling
400g (13 oz) pork mince
1 red chilli, seeded and chopped
2 teaspoons finely chopped ginger
1 clove garlic, crushed
2 tablespoons chopped coriander leaves
2 tablespoons soy sauce
dipping sauce
3 tablespoons hoi sin sauce*
2 tablespoons Chinese cooking (shao hsing) wine
2 teaspoons chopped ginger

Soak rice noodles in hot water until they are soft and pliable.
To make filling, combine pork, chilli, ginger, garlic, coriander and soy sauce in a bowl and mix well to combine.
Take ⅓ cup of filling and roll it into a long sausage to fit rice noodle rolls. Place filling at the end of the flat rice noodle and roll up to enclose. Repeat, using filling and rolls. Place rolls on a plate in a steamer and steam over a saucepan of boiling water for 5–6 minutes or until filling is cooked through. Serve with dipping sauce.
To make dipping sauce, place hoi sin sauce, wine and ginger in a saucepan and heat until simmering. Pour sauce into small bowls and serve with pork rolls. Serves 4 to 6 as a starter.

spinach with sesame and soy

500g (1 lb) English spinach leaves
sesame dressing
⅓ cup sesame seeds
4 tablespoons soy sauce
1 tablespoon sugar
4 tablespoons mirin

Place spinach in a saucepan of boiling water and cook for 10–15 seconds, drain and place under cold running water to cool.
To make sesame dressing, place sesame seeds in a dry frypan and toast until they are golden. Place sesame seeds and 1 tablespoon of soy sauce in a mortar and crush with the pestle until sesame seeds are a smooth paste. Add remaining soy sauce, sugar and mirin, and mix to combine. Place dressing in a small saucepan over medium heat and bring to the boil. Simmer for 2 minutes or until dressing thickens.
Place spinach on serving plate and top with sesame dressing. Sprinkle with extra sesame seeds and serve. Serves 4 as a starter or side dish.

rice noodles with barbecue duck

agedashi tofu

lemon-steamed chicken salad

red miso simmered eggplant

rice noodles with barbecue duck

1 Chinese barbecue duck*
400g (13 oz) fresh flat rice noodles
2 teaspoons sesame oil
1 tablespoon oil
1 tablespoon shredded ginger
10 shallots, cut into quarters
300g (10 oz) baby bok choy, broken into leaves
1/2 cup (4 fl oz) chicken stock*
2 tablespoons soy sauce
1/4 cup (2 fl oz) Chinese cooking (shao hsing) wine or sherry

Chop duck into bite-sized pieces and remove as many bones as possible. Cut rice noodles into very wide strips and rinse under hot water. Heat oils in a wok or frypan. Add ginger and shallots and cook for 1 minute.
Add duck to pan and cook for 1 minute. Add bok choy, rice noodles, stock, soy sauce and wine, and cook for 3–4 minutes or until duck is heated through. Serves 4.

agedashi tofu

500g (1 lb) firm silken tofu, sliced
rice flour for dusting
oil for frying
1 sheet nori,* finely shredded
sauce
1 1/2 cups (12 fl oz) dashi broth*
2 tablespoons soy sauce
3 tablespoons mirin
1 teaspoon sugar
8 small fresh shiitake mushrooms*
1 spring onion, finely sliced

To make sauce, place dashi broth, soy sauce, mirin, sugar and mushrooms in a saucepan over low heat and allow to simmer for 3 minutes. Stir through spring onion.
Toss tofu lightly in rice flour and shake away excess. Heat oil in a saucepan over high heat. When oil is hot, deep fry tofu, a few pieces at a time, until it is golden. Drain tofu on absorbent paper.
To serve, place hot tofu in serving bowls and pour over sauce. Top with shredded nori and serve immediately. Serves 4 to 6 as a starter.

lemon-steamed chicken salad

2 lemons, sliced
4 chicken breast fillets
1 teaspoons Szechwan peppercorns,* roasted and crushed
salad
2 tablespoons Vietnamese mint, shredded
1/2 cup mint leaves
1/2 cup Thai basil leaves
100g (3 oz) snow pea shoots
2 red onions, finely sliced
2 red chillies, seeded and sliced
3 tablespoons lemon juice
2 tablespoons fish sauce
1 tablespoon palm or brown sugar
1 tablespoon soy sauce

Line a bamboo steamer with lemon slices. Top lemon with chicken and sprinkle chicken with peppercorns. Cover, place steamer over a saucepan of boiling water and cook for 3–5 minutes or until chicken is tender. Set aside to cool. Shred chicken into fine pieces with your fingers.
To make salad, combine mints, basil, snow pea shoots, onions and chillies in a large serving bowl. Place lemon juice, fish sauce, sugar and soy sauce in a small bowl and whisk to combine. Toss chicken and dressing through salad and serve. Serves 4.

red miso simmered eggplant

2–3 tablespoons oil
2 eggplants (aubergines), chopped
2 teaspoons finely shredded ginger
2 tablespoons red miso*
2 tablespoons soy sauce
2 tablespoons mirin
1 1/2 cups (12 fl oz) dashi broth*

Heat oil in a frypan or wok and cook eggplant (aubergine) pieces, a few at a time, until they are golden on both sides. Remove eggplant (aubergine) from pan and set aside.
Add ginger to frypan and cook for 1 minute. Add miso, soy sauce, mirin and dashi broth and bring to the boil. Add eggplant (aubergine) to sauce and allow to simmer for 4 minutes or until eggplant (aubergine) is soft and sauce has thickened. Serves 4 as a starter or side dish.

seared beef with soba

rice paper wrapped fish

wok-fried chicken with tamarind

seared beef with soba

noodles and broth

300g (10 oz) green tea soba noodles*
1 cup (8 fl oz) water
2 tablespoons soy sauce
3 tablespoons mirin
1 tablespoon sugar
2 tablespoons bonito flakes*
3 shallots, chopped

beef

3 tablespoons soy sauce, extra
1 tablespoon lemon juice
1 tablespoon mirin, extra
2 teaspoons sesame oil
500g (1 lb) eye fillet

To cook noodles, place them in a large saucepan of boiling water and stir. Allow water to come back to the boil and then add 1 cup (8 fl oz) cold water. Repeat this process 3 times or until noodles are soft, then drain and rinse noodles well under cold running water.

To make broth, place water, soy sauce, mirin and sugar in a saucepan and bring to the boil. Add bonito flakes and remove pan from heat. Set aside for 5 minutes, then strain mixture through a fine sieve.

Combine extra soy sauce, lemon juice, extra mirin and sesame oil, and pour over beef. Allow beef to marinate for 20 minutes.

To serve, toss noodles in strained broth with shallots, and place on serving plates. Cook beef on a hot grill or frypan for 1 minute on each side or until it is seared and warm inside. Slice beef thinly, place on top of noodles and serve. Serves 4.

wok-fried chicken with tamarind

50g (1¾ oz) piece tamarind pulp
1 cup (8 fl oz) boiling water
2 double chicken breasts (850g or 1 lb 11 oz) on the bone
3 tablespoons soy sauce
1 tablespoon sesame oil
rice flour for dusting
2 tablespoons vegetable oil
8 shallots, halved
1 tablespoon shredded ginger
1 cup (8 fl oz) chicken stock*
2 tablespoons oyster sauce
1 tablespoon palm sugar

Place tamarind pulp in a bowl and cover with boiling water. Mix well with a fork to release the tamarind flavour and allow to stand for 5 minutes, then strain through a fine strainer.

Cut chicken into pieces and marinate in combined soy sauce and sesame oil for 30 minutes. Reserve marinade. Toss chicken in rice flour and shake off excess. Heat vegetable oil in frypan or wok over high heat. Cook chicken, a few pieces at a time, until well browned and set aside. Add reserved marinade, shallots and ginger to pan and cook for 1 minute. Add stock, tamarind water, oyster sauce and sugar to pan. Bring sauce to the boil and simmer until it has reduced by half. Return chicken to pan and simmer for 4–5 minutes or until it is cooked through. Serve chicken in bowls with ready-made Chinese steamed buns and steamed greens. Serves 4.

Note: Chinese buns, ready to steam, are available in the freezer section of Asian grocery stores.

rice paper wrapped fish

800g (1 lb 10 oz) piece blue eye cod fillet
2 green chillies, chopped
1 tablespoon sesame oil
4 tablespoons chopped coriander
2 tablespoons chopped Thai basil
1 teaspoon cumin seeds
12 large rice paper rounds*
oil for frying
black sesame seeds*

Wash cod, pat dry on absorbent paper and cut into
12 pieces. Place chillies, sesame oil, coriander, basil and
cumin seeds in a spice grinder or mortar and pestle, and
grind until they form a rough paste. Spread paste over fish.
Brush rice papers with warm water and set aside for
4 minutes or until they are soft. Place a piece of fish on
each round, fold in sides and roll to enclose.
Heat a little oil in a frypan over medium heat. Cook fish
parcels for 2–3 minutes on each side or until rice paper is
golden and crisp, and fish is tender. Drain on absorbent
paper. Sprinkle fish with sesame seeds, and serve with
steamed Asian greens drizzled with oyster sauce and
steamed jasmine rice. Serves 4.

tea cup steamed coconut cakes

4 eggs
1/2 cup sugar
1/4 cup grated palm sugar
1 tablespoon of boiling water
1 1/4 cups self-raising (self-rising) flour
3 tablespoons desiccated coconut

Place eggs and sugar in the bowl of an electric mixer.
Combine palm sugar and water, mix until sugar has
dissolved, and add to eggs and sugar in bowl. Beat mixture
at high speed for 8–10 minutes or until it is light and thick.
Carefully fold through flour and coconut.
Spoon mixture into 6 Chinese tea cups or small rice bowls.
Place tea cups in a steamer over a wok of boiling water,
cover and steam for 15 minutes or until cakes are puffed
and firm. Serve with small pots of Chinese tea. Makes 6.

sticky rice with mango and lime

1 cup glutinous rice*
2 1/2 cups (20 fl oz) water
1/2 cup (4 fl oz) coconut cream
3 tablespoons sugar
6 x 15cm (6 inch) squares banana leaves
filling
1 mango, peeled and chopped
1 teaspoon grated lime rind
2 tablespoons lime juice
1 tablespoon grated palm sugar

Rinse rice well under cold water, then drain. Place rice and
water in a saucepan over medium heat and bring to the
boil. Allow rice to simmer until almost all liquid has been
absorbed. Remove pan from heat and pour coconut cream
over rice. Cover rice and allow to stand for 5–7 minutes or
until coconut cream has been absorbed. Stir sugar through
rice and set aside.
Place banana leaves in boiling water for 1–2 minutes or until
they are soft. Divide rice into 6 portions. Spread half of each
portion over the middle of the banana leaf. Top rice with a
sprinkling of mango, lime rind and juice, and palm sugar.
Cover filling with remaining portion of rice.
Roll up leaves and secure with toothpicks. Place leaf
packages on a hot barbecue or char grill and cook for
2 minutes on each side or until rice is heated through.
Serve warm or cold. Serves 6.

steamed palm sugar custards

3 cups milk
1/3 cup palm sugar
1 star anise
1 cinnamon stick
2 eggs

Place milk, sugar, star anise and cinnamon in a saucepan
over low heat for 5 minutes. Strain mixture and place in a
bowl. Beat eggs lightly and whisk into milk mixture.
Pour mixture into 6–8 Chinese tea cups and place tea cups
in a steamer. Place steamer over rapidly simmering water
for 20 minutes or until custards are just set. Serves 6 to 8.

tea cup steamed coconut cakes

sticky rice with mango and lime

steamed palm sugar custards

menu ideas

dim sum lunch for 6

pork rice noodle rolls
prawn and chilli pot-sticker dumplings
rice paper wrapped fish
rice noodles with barbecue duck*
tea cup steamed coconut cakes

FOOD PREP
For starters, serve the pork rice noodle rolls and the prawn and chilli pot-sticker dumplings with bowls of chilli jam on the side. Both of these can be prepared ahead of time and steamed when required. For mains, serve the rice paper wrapped fish, which you can prepare beforehand and cook just before serving, and small bowls of the rice noodles with barbecue duck.* Finish with the tea cup steamed coconut cakes, which can be made 1 day in advance and refrigerated until required.

LIQUID SUGGESTIONS
The obvious choice would be a pot of Chinese tea such as jasmine or chrysanthemum tea. If you wish to drink wine, choose a young rielsing to complement the chilli and spice.

asian banquet for 8

spinach with sesame and soy
red miso* simmered eggplant
lemon-steamed chicken salad
seared beef with soba
steamed palm sugar custards

FOOD PREP
Start with a few dishes such as the spinach with sesame and soy (x 2), which is easily prepared a few hours beforehand, and the red miso* simmered eggplant (aubergine) (x 2). Prepare the lemon-steamed chicken salad and refrigerate until required, and serve it with the seared beef with soba. Finish with the velvety steamed palm sugar custards, which can be steamed 1 day in advance and refrigerated until serving.

LIQUID SUGGESTIONS
A big pot of Chinese tea would be great. This menu also suits a dry cold beer, a riesling or a sauvignon blanc.

japanese dinner for 6

agedashi tofu
spinach with sesame and soy
vinegared rice box with marinated sashimi
seared beef with soba
sticky rice with mango and lime

FOOD PREP
Start with the well-flavoured agedashi tofu and the spinach with sesame and soy (x 1½). The spinach can be prepared a few hours beforehand. Move on to vinegared rice boxes with marinated sashimi (x 1½) and the seared beef with soba (x 1½). Remember to allow time for the sashimi marinade to stand. Even though sticky rice with mango and lime is not particularly Japanese, you can make it beforehand and steam it when required. If time is short, serve ready-made green tea ice cream.

LIQUID SUGGESTIONS
A warmed or chilled sake works well with Japanese food. Check the bottle to see whether the type of sake you are buying is for drinking warm or chilled. You could also serve Japanese green tea or a dry Japanese beer.

morsels with drinks for 10

spinach with sesame and soy
agedashi tofu
prawn and chilli pot-sticker dumplings
rice paper wrapped fish
lemon-steamed chicken salad

FOOD PREP
Spinach with sesame and soy and agedashi tofu can be served in Chinese soup spoons. Both can be prepared ahead of time. Deep fry the tofu just before serving. Serve dumplings on a platter with small bowls of chilli jam. Rice paper wrapped fish can be made into smaller bite-sized pieces and lemon steamed chicken salad can be served in individual baby cos lettuce leaves.

LIQUID SUGGESTIONS
Hand around small bottles of chilled sake, or shot glasses of warm sake. See drinks chapter for cocktail suggestions.

garden
lunch

3

basics

Fruits, vegetables and herbs are best purchased, cooked and eaten when they are in season. At the height of their season, they have the maximum flavour and are probably at their best price. Growing seasons are being extended all the time with new varieties of fruits and vegetables and, with the help of modern transport, seasonal produce is often available for longer periods. Use the following loose guide for a few of your favourites.

any time

As a result of advanced growing techniques, many more fruits and vegetables are available year round. These include beetroots, capsicums (peppers), eggplants (aubergines) and sweet potatoes.

summer

From the heady aroma of basil to succulent stone fruits, summer is the perfect time for the fruit and berry lover. To prolong your enjoyment of summer stone fruits, preserve them in a light sugar syrup or make them into jams and chutneys for the colder months ahead. Summer favourites include basil, berries, corn, cucumbers, figs, garlic, lettuce, peas, new potatoes, salad greens, snake beans, stone fruits, tomatoes and zucchini (courgettes).

spring

Burst in to spring with an amazing variety of delicate green vegetables. Lightly blanch tender young spring greens for simple, fresh salads. Spring produce includes Asian greens, asparagus, beans, broad (fava) beans, carrots, globe artichokes, peas, rocket (arugula) and spinach.

autumn

Autumn, the mellow season, is a time to prepare for the colder months. Warming pasta dishes and risotto help the transition to winter. Try mushrooms, okra, olives, onions pumpkin and spinach during autumn.

winter

Winter is a great time for soups and slowly simmered dishes that contain hearty root vegetables and winter-cropping members of the brassica family. Look out for blood oranges, broccoli, brussel sprouts, cabbage, cauliflower, celeriac, fennel, Jerusalem artichokes, leeks, parsnips, potatoes, persimmons and quinces during the winter months.

any time

winter

spring

autumn

summer

53

marinated sheep's yoghurt cheese

fennel and mushroom salad

marinated beets   seared scallops on lemon and mint salad

marinated sheep's yoghurt cheese

1kg (2 lb) sheep's milk yoghurt
1 tablespoon sea salt
2 teaspoons cracked black pepper
2 tablespoons chopped lemon thyme
1 red chilli, seeded and chopped

Combine yoghurt, salt, pepper, thyme and chilli, and pour mixture into a bowl lined with a double layer of cheesecloth. Tie ends of cheesecloth together. Suspend cheesecloth bundle from a shelf in the refrigerator and place a bowl underneath, to collect drips, for 24–48 hours or until yoghurt mixture is firm.
Remove yoghurt from cheesecloth and shape it into small balls. Place balls on a tray, cover loosely and refrigerate for 3–4 hours or until yoghurt balls become firm. Slice yoghurt cheese balls and serve on grilled bread. Use within 3 days or store cheese balls whole, covered in olive oil, in a sterilised jar in the refrigerator. Makes 10 balls.

fennel and mushroom salad

4 large field mushrooms
2 tablespoons butter, melted
1 tablespoon oil
150g (5 oz) baby English spinach leaves
1 tablespoon sage leaves
1 tablespoon shredded lemon rind
2 baby fennel bulbs, thinly sliced
1/2 cup marinated green olives
cracked black pepper
2 tablespoons balsamic vinegar

Wipe mushrooms clean and trim stems. Brush mushrooms with butter and oil, and place on a hot preheated grill. Cook mushrooms for 2 minutes on each side.
To serve, place a pile of baby spinach leaves on each serving plate. Scatter sage leaves and lemon rind over spinach and top with a mushroom. Top with fennel, olives and pepper. Drizzle balsamic vinegar over salad and serve with warm sourdough bread. Serves 4 as a starter.

marinated beets

18 baby beetroots, peeled and trimmed
2 cups (16 fl oz) white wine vinegar
1 cup (8 fl oz) water
1/2 cup sugar
1 tablespoon coriander seeds
2 tablespoons orange rind strips
2 tablespoons dill sprigs

Place beetroots in a saucepan of boiling water and cook for 6 minutes or until they are tender, then drain and peel. Place vinegar, water, sugar, coriander seeds and orange rind strips in a non-reactive saucepan* and bring mixture to the boil. Remove pan from heat and add beetroot and dill. Allow mixture to cool. Store beets and marinade in sterilised jars in the refrigerator. Marinated beets are great served with washed-rind cheese and bread. Makes 1 medium jar.

seared scallops on lemon and mint salad

24 scallops
cracked black pepper
olive oil
2 teaspoons grated lemon rind
salad
2 cups mint leaves
1/2 cup Vietnamese mint leaves
1 bunch (100g or 31/2 oz) rocket (arugula) leaves
1/4 cup (2 fl oz) lemon juice
1 red chilli, seeded and chopped
2 teaspoons grated ginger
1 tablespoon vegetable oil

Combine scallops with a little pepper, olive oil and lemon rind and set aside for 5 minutes.
Combine mints and rocket (arugula) and arrange on serving plates. Combine lemon juice, chilli, ginger and oil.
Preheat a frypan over high heat. Add scallops to pan and cook for 10 seconds on each side or until they are seared. Place scallops on salad and pour over lemon dressing. Serves 4 to 6 as a starter.

pickled spring onions

24 small brown or spring pickling onions
5 cups (40 fl oz) white wine vinegar
6 tablespoons sugar
1 teaspoon cumin seeds
8 sprigs dill
4 sprigs marjoram
4 red chillies, halved and seeds removed
1 teaspoon black peppercorns

Peel and trim onions, and set aside. Place vinegar and sugar in a non-reactive saucepan* and bring mixture to the boil. Once vinegar boils, add onions, cumin seeds, dill, marjoram, chillies and peppercorns. Simmer for 6–8 minutes or until onions are soft. Pour into a sterilised jar and seal jar with a non-metallic lid. Allow onions to stand for at least 2 days before serving. Makes 1 large jar.

parmesan and sorrel grilled witlof

4 witlof (chicory), halved
sea salt
1 cup young sorrel leaves
1/4 cup flat-leaf (Italian) parsley
3 tablespoons lemon juice
1 tablespoon sugar
cracked black pepper
1/2 cup grated parmesan cheese

Bring a saucepan of water to the boil, and add witlof and a little salt to pan. Cook for 4 minutes or until witlof are tender, then drain well.
Place sorrel and parsley leaves between witlof leaves. Place witlof on a baking tray and sprinkle with lemon juice, sugar, pepper and parmesan. Place witlof under a preheated hot grill and cook for 4–6 minutes or until they are golden.
Serve grilled witlof with slices of smoked salmon and salad greens. Serves 4.

asparagus with herb brown butter sauce

750g (1½ lb) asparagus, trimmed and halved
90g (3 oz) butter
cracked black pepper
2 tablespoons sage leaves
2 tablespoons oregano leaves
2 tablespoons marjoram leaves
1 tablespoon lemon juice
chilli pasta to serve
parmesan shavings to serve

Place asparagus in a steamer or in boiling water and cook until it is tender, then drain.
To make herb brown butter sauce, place butter, pepper, sage, oregano and marjoram in a saucepan over medium heat and cook for 4–6 minutes or until butter is golden brown. Remove pan from heat and add lemon juice.
Place asparagus on a pile of chilli pasta. Spoon herb brown butter over pasta and asparagus, and serve with shavings of parmesan cheese. Serves 6 as a starter or 4 as a main meal.

pear, ginger and chilli chutney

1 kg (2 lb) pears, peeled, cored and chopped
1/4 cup shredded ginger
6 red chillies, seeded and chopped
2 onions, finely chopped
3 tablespoons chopped coriander
2 kaffir lime* leaves
2½ cups (20 fl oz) cider vinegar
1 cup brown sugar
1 cup white sugar
cracked black pepper and sea salt

Place pears, ginger, chillies, onions, coriander, kaffir lime leaves, vinegar and sugars in a non-reactive saucepan* over high heat. Bring mixture to the boil, then reduce heat to simmer and cook for 30 minutes or until chutney is thick, stirring occasionally and skimming the surface. Taste chutney before adding pepper and salt.
Pour chutney into sterilised jars and seal. Serve chutney on sandwiches or with grilled or roast meats. Makes 1 large jar.

pickled spring onions

asparagus with herb brown butter sauce

parmesan and sorrel grilled witlof

pear, ginger and chilli chutney

green pea broth

filled tomatoes & (right) basil-rubbed toasts

green pea broth

2 smoked ham hocks, halved
3 litres (96 fl oz) water
1½ cups (12 fl oz) dry white wine
12 pearl or small brown onions
3 bay leaves
1 teaspoon peppercorns
2 cups fresh peas
1 cup shredded celeriac or parsnip
1 tablespoon mint leaves
1 tablespoon chervil sprigs

Remove skin and any visible fat from hocks. Place hocks in a large stockpot with water, wine, onions, bay leaves and peppercorns. Bring liquid to the boil, then cover and simmer for 1 hour. Strain stock through a fine sieve. Remove onions from pot, and wash and halve them. Chop meat from bones and place in a clean saucepan with onions.
Add strained stock to pan and bring to the boil. Add peas and celeriac to pan and simmer for 5 minutes or until vegetables are tender. Ladle soup into bowls and sprinkle with mint and chervil. Serve with grilled bread. Serves 4 to 6 as a starter.

filled tomatoes with basil-rubbed toasts

4 ripe beefsteak or garden tomatoes
4 bocconcini or 300g (10 oz) smoked mozzarella, sliced
⅓ cup shaved parmesan cheese
½ cup basil leaves
½ cup (4 fl oz) balsamic vinegar
3 tablespoons extra virgin olive oil
2 teaspoons brown sugar
sea salt and cracked black pepper
mixed salad greens
basil-rubbed toasts
12 slices crusty Italian bread
olive oil, extra
1 large bunch basil

Cut slits almost completely through tomatoes, leaving bases intact. Fill slits with bocconcini or mozzarella, parmesan and basil. Combine balsamic vinegar, olive oil, sugar, and salt and pepper, and pour over tomatoes. Allow tomatoes to stand for at least 20 minutes.
To make basil-rubbed toasts, brush bread with extra olive oil and toast under griller until slices are golden brown on both sides. Take a large handful of basil leaves and rub them into one side of the warm pieces of toast.
To serve, place greens on serving plates and top with tomatoes. Serve tomatoes with warm basil-rubbed toasts and lots of cracked pepper. Serves 4.

summer fruits free-form pie

1 quantity (350g or 11¼ oz) sweet shortcrust pastry*
milk
demerara sugar
filling
2 peaches, sliced
200g (6½ oz) raspberries
3 plums, sliced
200g (6½ oz) blueberries
1 tablespoon flour

Roll out pastry on a lightly floured surface until it is 3mm (⅛ inch) thick. Place pastry in a 23cm (9 inch) pie dish, leaving an 8–10cm (3–4 inch) overhang, and refrigerate until required.
To make filling, combine peaches, raspberries, plums, blueberries and flour. Pile fruit mixture into pie base. Fold over excess pastry to partly encase fruit. Refrigerate pie for 20 minutes or until pastry is firm. Brush pastry with a little milk and sprinkle pie well with sugar.
Bake pie in a preheated 200°C (400°F) oven for 20 minutes or until pastry is golden and fruit is tender. Serve pie warm or cold with clotted cream. Serves 8 to 10.
Note: when making pastry for this pie, use 30g (1 oz) less butter and more iced water to make pastry firmer.

sour lemon cake

125g (4 oz) butter
¾ cup caster (superfine) sugar
1½ tablespoons grated lemon rind
2 eggs, lightly beaten
1½ cups self-raising (self-rising) flour
½ cup sour cream
½ cup (4 fl oz) lemon juice

Place butter, sugar and lemon rind in the bowl of an electric mixer, and beat until light and creamy. Add eggs to mixer and beat well. Fold flour, sour cream and lemon juice through mixture.
Immediately place mixture in a greased and lined 20cm (8 inch) square cake tin and bake in a preheated 180°C (350°F) oven for 40 minutes or until cake is cooked when tested with a skewer.
Cut cake into wedges and serve warm with cream. Serves 8 to 10.

sour lemon cake

summer fruits free-form pie

menu ideas

sunday lunch for 4

marinated beets
seared scallops on lemon and mint salad
summer fruits free-form pie

FOOD PREP
Prepare marinated beets up to 3–4 days before serving them with washed-rind cheese and crusty bread. Follow this with scallop salad. Prepare the salad the morning before serving and sear scallops just before serving. Serve summer fruits free-from pie for dessert with clotted cream. The pie can be made in the morning before your guests arrive.

LIQUID SUGGESTIONS
Serve an aged semillon or chardonnay with the beets. The flavour of the scallops would be good with a semillon or sauvignon blanc. Serve the pie with your choice of sweet wine or a lazy-afternoon glass of port and coffee.

mezze lunch for 6

marinated beets
marinated sheep's yoghurt cheese
pickled spring onions
parmesan and sorrel grilled witlof (chicory)
seared scallops on lemon and mint salad
sour lemon cake

FOOD PREP
Most of this lunch can be prepared well in advance. Have a large table layed out with marinated beets, yoghurt cheese, pickled onions, grilled witlof (chicory) and a platter of scallops on lemon and mint salad. This allows people to pick and choose. Be sure to serve plenty of bread and some extra cheeses to round out the table. Make lemon cake the day before and store it in an airtight container. When you are ready to serve, cut it into wedges and serve cake with thick cream, to complete a perfect lunch.

LIQUID SUGGESTIONS
With all the full-flavoured marinated goodies, serve a lightly wooded chardonnay as your white wine and a well-flavoured pinot noir as your red. The cake is a treat with an apple- or pear-infused brandy and strong coffee.

light spring lunch for 8

fennel and mushroom salad
asparagus with herb brown butter sauce

FOOD PREP
Start with the fennel and mushroom salad (x 2) with some flatbreads on the side. Follow this with the asparagus with herb brown butter sauce (x 1½–2) nestled on a mound of chilli pasta. For dessert, serve a plate of fresh fruits sprinkled with lime and palm sugar or a drizzle of botrytis-affected riesling.

LIQUID SUGGESTIONS
Try sparkling spring water flavoured with lemon thyme and lime wedges or a fresh fruit cordial (see portable food). If wine is your wish, a crisp sauvignon blanc would be perfect.

formal garden lunch for 10

green pea broth
filled tomatoes with basil-rubbed toasts
asparagus with herb brown butter sauce
summer fruits free-form pie

FOOD PREP
Start with the green pea broth (x 2), which can be prepared ahead of time and gently warmed before serving. Then serve a starter of filled tomatoes with basil-rubbed toasts (x 2), which can be prepared a few hours beforehand. Follow these with asparagus with herb brown butter sauce (x 2) and finish with a summer fruits free-form pie with vanilla bean ice cream. Prepare the pastry for the pie the day before and refrigerate it until you are ready to roll pastry and make pie.

LIQUID SUGGESTIONS
A sparkling white wine, a refreshing riesling or a clean sauvignon blanc will suit the green pea broth and a chardonnay goes well with the tomatoes. Continue with the chardonnay or offer a spicy pinot noir with the asparagus. Accompany the pie with a chilled late-cut riesling and coffees.

grill

grill

basics

There are many different sites where you can grill foods, from the traditional backyard barbecue to the grill pan on your cooktop or the electric char grill. As there are now many indoor grilling options, this method of cooking is not only for the warm, fine-weather months. Indoor grilling is best done in a well-ventilated kitchen.

herb brushes

To avoid melting a normal kitchen basting brush, use a bunch of herbs tied with string to dip in the cooking oil and brush the grill or barbecue. To reduce the amount of smoke from the grill (especially if you are grilling inside), brush the food not the grill. Use sturdy herbs such as rosemary, thyme, lemon thyme, oregano or marjoram.

barbecues

These come in many different varieties. Some have grills and flat plates combined with volcanic rocks, heat beads or coals. Woodchips or smoking chips are great for home smoking in covered barbecues. Barbecues are handy for cooking large fish and covered barbecues are great for large roasts. It'll keep the heat out of the kitchen during summer.

char grills

Electric char grills or in-bench gas or electric grills are great alternatives to the backyard barbecue. When using these inside, remember to open the window or turn on the exhaust fan.

tongs

If you are grilling a substantial amount of food over high heat, use long-handled tongs for flipping sausages, steaks, fish and burgers on the barbecue or grill. Avoid leaving tongs on a hot surface as they heat up quickly.

grill pans

These are great for use indoors, and they are sometimes more convenient than outdoor barbecues. Grill pans come in flat-plate as well as frypan varieties for use on the stove top. Flat-plate grills often cover two elements on the stove top, so check the size before purchasing one. They are mostly available in cast iron but a few are made of a lighter steel with a non-stick coating.

grill pan

char grill

herb brush

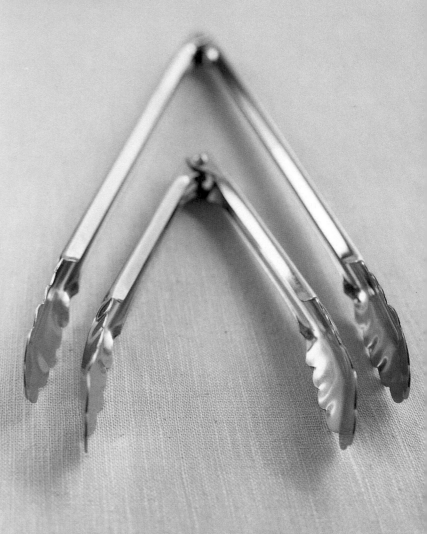

tongs

barbecue

smoked eggplant and white bean pûrée & rosemary and sea-salt grilled flatbreads

swordfish grilled with vine leaves

smoked eggplant and white bean pûrée

2 eggplants (aubergines)
2 cloves garlic, unpeeled
1 cup cooked cannellini beans
1/3 cup (2¾ fl oz) olive oil
1 tablespoon tahini
1/4 teaspoon ground cumin
1/4 cup (2 fl oz) lemon juice
2 tablespoons chopped flat-leaf (Italian) parsley
1 tablespoon chopped mint
sea salt and pepper

Place eggplants (aubergines) and garlic on a preheated hot grill and cook for 6–8 minutes or until skins are well charred and flesh is soft. Peel skins from eggplant and garlic, and place flesh in a food processor or blender with beans, oil, tahini, cumin and lemon juice, and process until smooth. Stir parsley, mint, and salt and pepper through pûrée. Serve with warm grilled bread. Serves 6 to 8 as a starter.

grilled eggplant and mint salad

2 eggplants (aubergines), sliced
2 small fennel bulbs, sliced
2 zucchini (courgettes), sliced
olive oil
150g (5 oz) haloumi,* sliced
1/2 cup shredded mint
3 tablespoons lemon juice
2 tablespoons chopped flat-leaf (Italian) parsley
1 tablespoon honey
cracked black pepper

Brush slices of eggplant (aubergine), fennel and zucchini (courgette) with a little olive oil, place on a hot preheated grill and grill for 1–2 minutes on each side or until they are soft. Brush haloumi slices with a little oil, place on a flat grill or hot frypan and cook for 1 minute on each side or until haloumi is golden.
Arrange grilled vegetables and haloumi on serving plates and sprinkle with mint. Combine lemon juice, parsley, honey and pepper, and pour dressing over salad. Serve with bread. Serves 4 to 6 as a starter.

swordfish grilled with vine leaves

4 swordfish steaks
2 teaspoons grated lemon rind
1 clove garlic, crushed
2 tablespoons finely chopped flat-leaf (Italian) parsley
2 tablespoons olive oil
8 fresh vine leaves or leaves in brine
olive oil, extra

Trim swordfish skin, wash and pat fish dry. Combine lemon rind, garlic, parsley and olive oil, and brush over both sides of fish. Place a vine leaf on each side of the fish and tuck in ends to secure. Place fish on a tray and brush leaves with a little oil.
Place tray under a hot grill and cook for 2–3 minutes on each side or until fish is tender. Serve fish with a spinach salad and wedges of lemon. Serves 4.

rosemary and sea-salt grilled flatbreads

1 teaspoon active dry yeast
2½ cups (20 fl oz) warm water
3½ cups wholemeal plain (all-purpose) flour
2 teaspoons sea salt
1 tablespoon olive oil
2½ –3 cups plain (all-purpose) flour
topping
olive oil
sea salt
rosemary leaves

Dissolve yeast and water in a bowl. Place wholemeal flour in the bowl of an electric mixer fitted with a dough hook. Alternatively, use a bowl and wooden spoon instead of dough hook. Add yeast mixture to bowl and mix until well combined. Cover mixture with plastic wrap and allow it to stand in a warm place for 1 hour or until doubled in size. Add sea salt and oil to bowl of mixer and beat with dough hook until combined. While motor is running, gradually add plain flour until a soft dough forms. When dough forms, allow the dough hook to knead it for 8 minutes. Cover dough with plastic wrap and allow it to double in size (this takes about 2 hours).
Divide dough into 16 pieces and roll each piece into a ball. Roll out balls on a lightly floured surface until they are 4mm (1/4 inch) thick. Brush one side of dough with a little olive oil, and sprinkle with salt and rosemary leaves. Allow dough to rise for 10 minutes.
Cook flatbreads on a preheated hot grill or barbecue for 1 minute on each side or until they are puffed and golden. Serve warm. Makes 16.

grilled eggplant and mint salad

spicy rocket beef sausage

beef burgers with fried tomatoes and chillies

chilli salt and pepper squid

kaffir salmon with grilled limes

coriander prawns with honey bok choy

beef burgers with fried tomatoes and chillies

500g (1 lb) minced beef
2 tablespoons Worcestershire sauce
1 clove garlic, crushed
2 tablespoons Dijon mustard
2 tablespoons chopped coriander
1 onion, sliced
2 green tomatoes, sliced
2 mild green chillies, sliced
2 tablespoons oil
salad greens
4 bread rolls, halved and toasted

Combine beef, Worcestershire sauce, garlic, mustard and coriander. Divide mixture into 4 and shape into patties. Place patties and onion slices on a hot preheated grill. Place tomatoes and chillies on a hot grill. Brush oil over onion, tomatoes and chillies. Cook patties, onion, tomatoes and chillies for 3 minutes on each side or until vegetables are well browned and patties are cooked through. Place salad greens on bottom half of bread rolls. Top greens with onions, patties, tomatoes and chillies. Cover with top of roll and serve. Serves 4.

spicy rocket beef sausage

750g (1½ lb) sausage mince
250g (8 oz) minced beef
2 cups shredded rocket (arugula)
3 tablespoons seeded mustard
1 clove garlic, crushed
2 tablespoons chopped thyme
cracked black pepper
sausage skins

Combine sausage mince, minced beef, rocket (arugula), mustard, garlic, thyme and pepper. Place mixture in a piping bag fitted with a large plain nozzle.
Slide sausage skin over nozzle of piping bag and gather skin over nozzle until you reach the end. Pipe mixture into sausage skin, allowing sausage skin to slide from the nozzle as you pipe. Twist sausage at regular intervals to form indivdual sausages. Place sausages in refrigerator for 4 hours or overnight.
To cook, place sausages in a saucepan of cold water. Slowly bring the water to a simmer, then remove pan from heat and drain sausages. Cook sausages on a medium hot preheated grill or barbecue until they are cooked through. Serve with a spicy chutney and grilled onion. Serves 4 to 6.

chilli salt and pepper squid

3 red chillies, seeded and chopped
1 tablespoon sea-salt flakes
1 teaspoon cracked black pepper
12 baby or small squid, cleaned and halved
2 tablespoons oil
100g (3½ oz) rice vermicelli
3 tablespoons soy sauce
2 tablespoons lime juice
3 tablespoons coriander leaves
1 tablespoon brown sugar
2 teaspoons fish sauce

Combine chillies, and salt and pepper in a bowl. Brush squid lightly with oil and press in chilli mixture to coat both sides, then set aside.
Place rice vermicelli in a bowl and pour over boiling water. Allow vermicelli to stand for 5 minutes or until it is tender, then drain. Toss vermicelli with soy sauce, lime juice, coriander, sugar and fish sauce. Divide vermicelli between serving bowls.
To cook squid, preheat a grill or frypan over high heat. Cook squid for 10–15 seconds on each side. Place squid on top of vermicelli and serve. Serves 4.

kaffir salmon with grilled limes

4 kaffir lime* leaves, shredded
2 tablespoons lime juice
2 teaspoons grated ginger
2 teaspoons sesame oil
2 teaspoons chilli oil
4 x 185g (6 oz) pieces salmon fillet
4 limes, halved
salad greens to serve

Combine lime leaves, lime juice, ginger, and sesame and chilli oils, and pour over salmon. Allow salmon to marinate for 10 minutes. Place salmon and limes, flesh side down, on a preheated hot grill and cook for 1 minute on each side or until they are cooked to your liking. Serve salmon with salad greens tossed in a light lemon dressing. Serves 4.

balsamic marinated steak

herb chicken skewers

coriander prawns with honey bok choy

750g (1½ lb) large green (raw) prawns
¼ cup chopped coriander
2 tablespoons lime juice
2 teaspoons sesame oil
1 green chilli, seeded and chopped
1 tablespoon chopped mint
honey bok choy
400g (13 oz) baby bok choy
3 tablespoons honey
3 tablespoons Chinese cooking (shao hsing) wine
1 tablespoon sesame seeds
3 tablespoons oyster sauce

Remove heads from prawns, peel, devein and leave tails intact. Place each prawn on a skewer. Combine coriander, lime juice, sesame oil, chilli and mint, and pour over prawns. Allow prawns to marinate for at least 10 minutes.
To make honey bok choy, place bok choy in a saucepan of boiling water and cook for 30 seconds, then drain. Place honey, wine, sesame seeds and oyster sauce in a frypan over medium heat and allow to simmer. Add bok choy to pan and cook for 1 minute.
To cook prawns, place them on a hot barbecue, char grill or frypan and cook for 1–2 minutes on each side or until they are just cooked. To serve, place bok choy on serving plates and top with prawns. Serves 4 to 6 as a starter.

balsamic marinated steak

4 steaks (fillet, New York or Scotch fillet)
salad greens
marinade
⅓ cup (2¾ oz) balsamic vinegar
⅓ cup (2¾ oz) olive oil
2 tablespoons shredded basil
1 teaspoon cracked black pepper
2 pieces lemon rind
2 cloves garlic, sliced

Trim steak of excess fat. To make marinade, combine balsamic vinegar, oil, basil, pepper, lemon rind and garlic. Place steak in marinade and allow to marinate for at least 30 minutes.
To cook steak, preheat a char grill, barbecue or frypan over very high heat. Cook steaks, ensuring they are sealed well, until they are cooked to your liking. To serve, pile salad greens onto serving plates and top with grilled steaks. Serves 4.

herb chicken skewers

4 chicken breast fillets
¼ cup rosemary sprigs
¼ cup oregano sprigs
10 mild red chillies, halved and seeded
3 tablespoons lemon juice
3 tablespoons soy sauce
2 teaspoons sesame oil
2 cloves garlic, crushed
2 teaspoons grated ginger
1 tablespoon brown sugar

Cut chicken into thick strips. Thread chicken onto skewers with sprigs of rosemary, oregano and chillies. Combine lemon juice, soy sauce, sesame oil, garlic, ginger and sugar, and pour over skewers. Allow chicken to marinate for 20 minutes.
To cook, place chicken skewers on a hot grill and cook for 2 minutes on each side or until meat is cooked through. Serve with salad greens. Serves 4.

lemon and szechwan pepper sardines

12 fresh sardines, butterflied
2 parsnips, peeled
oil for deep frying
sea salt
marinade
3 tablespoons lemon juice
2 tablespoons Szechwan peppercorns,* toasted and crushed
2 tablespoons olive oil
2 tablespoons Thai basil, shredded

Wash sardines and pat them dry. To make marinade, combine lemon juice, peppercorns, olive oil and basil. Pour marinade over sardines and allow to marinate for 20 minutes.
Cut parsnips into thin strips. In a saucepan, heat oil for deep frying. Cook parsnip strips, a few at a time, until they are golden and crisp. Drain chips on absorbent paper and keep them warm in a warm oven.
To cook sardines, preheat a grill, barbecue or frypan over high heat. Cook sardines for 1–2 minutes on each side or until they are tender. Place parsnip chips on serving plates, top with salt and sardines, and serve. Serves 4 as a starter.

lemon and szechwan pepper sardines

tequila lime and ruby grapefruit sorbet   grilled mango with coconut praline

tequila lime and ruby grapefruit sorbet

1 cup (8 fl oz) lime juice
1 tablespoon finely grated lime rind
1¼ cups sugar
3 cups (24 fl oz) bottled ruby grapefruit juice
⅓ cup (2¾ fl oz) tequila

Place lime juice, lime rind and sugar in a saucepan. Stir mixture over low heat until sugar has dissolved. Pour ruby grapefruit juice, sugar mixture and tequila into a bowl and stir to combine. Pour mixture into an ice-cream maker and follow manufacturer's instructions to make sorbet. Alternatively, pour mixture into a bowl and freeze for 1 hour. Whisk sorbet and freeze for another hour. Whisk sorbet again and freeze until it is solid. Serve sorbet in scoops. Serves 6.

pears with maple syrup yoghurt

2 pears, sliced
60g (2 oz) butter, melted
⅓ cup demerara sugar
1 cup thick yoghurt
¼ cup (2 fl oz) maple syrup

Brush pears with butter and sprinkle with demerara sugar. Place pear slices on a hot preheated flat grill or frypan and cook for 1 minute on each side or until they are golden. To serve, stack slices of pear on serving plates. Top pears with a spoonful of yoghurt and drizzle with maple syrup. Serves 4.

grilled mango with coconut praline

2 mangoes
1 tablespoon lime juice
coconut praline
1 cup sugar
½ cup (4 fl oz) water
1 cup toasted shredded coconut

To make coconut praline, place sugar and water in a saucepan over low heat and stir until sugar has dissolved. Allow sugar syrup to rapidly simmer for 5–7 minutes or until liquid is a light golden colour. Spread coconut on a baking tray and pour over hot sugar mixture to cover. Allow praline to stand for 5 minutes or until it is hard. Break coconut praline into small pieces.
Slice cheeks from mangoes and brush them with lime juice. Place mango cheeks on a hot preheated grill, flesh side down, and grill for 3 minutes or until they are golden and warm.
To serve, place mango on serving plates and serve with the coconut praline. Serves 4.

pears with maple syrup yoghurt

menu ideas

barbecue for 8

chilli salt and pepper squid
herb chicken skewers
balsamic marinated steak
grilled eggplant (aubergine) and mint salad
tequila lime and ruby grapefruit sorbet

FOOD PREP
Two dishes make a great informal starter: the chilli salt and pepper squid and the herb chicken skewers. Prepare these beforehand, refrigerate and barbecue when required. Marinate steaks (x 2) up to 2 hours before barbecuing and the grilled eggplant (aubergine) and mint salad (x 2) can be prepared ahead of time too. Serve mains with a bowl of salad greens, and a selection of mustards and chutneys. Finish with the tequila lime and ruby grapefruit sorbet, which can be made up to 2 days ahead or time.

LIQUID SUGGESTIONS
Lots of cold water, still or sparkling, is great when you are sitting around outdoors in the sun. Some say you can't really go past a good ice-cold beer at a barbecue, but if you can, try a riesling or sauvignon blanc with the starters and a cabernet sauvignon or well-flavoured, spicy chilled pinot noir with the steaks. For the wild at heart, a few cold shots of tequila with the sorbet won't go astray.

seaside dinner for 4

lemon and szechwan pepper* sardines
swordfish grilled with vine leaves
grilled mango with coconut praline

FOOD PREP
Start with the great textures and flavours of the lemon and szechwan pepper* sardines. Follow this with the swordfish grilled with vine leaves and some green salad leaves dressed in lemon and olive oil. The swordfish can be prepared ahead of time and barbecued when required. Finish with grilled mango with coconut praline. You can make the coconut praline ahead of time and store it in an airtight container away from moisture.

LIQUID SUGGESTIONS
Some of the new fruit- and herb-infused mineral waters are nice to start with. The rich sardines are great with an aged semillon or lightly wooded chardonnay. Stick to the semillon, or change to a dry riesling with the swordfish, and finish with a sweet, floral dessert wine and coffee.

al fresco evening grill for 6

rosemary and sea-salt grilled flatbreads
smoked eggplant (aubergine) and white bean pûrée
coriander prawns with honey bok choy
kaffir salmon with grilled limes
tequila lime and ruby grapefruit sorbet

FOOD PREP
Start with the rosemary and sea-salt grilled flatbreads with the smoked eggplant (aubergine) and white bean pûrée. Make the pûrée and the flatbread dough ahead of time. Place the rolled flatbread dough in the freezer to stop the yeast over proving* the bread. Small servings of the coriander prawns with honey bok choy make good starters and then move on to the kaffir salmon with grilled limes (x 1½). Finish with the tequila lime and ruby grapefruit sorbet, which can be made up to 2 days in advance. To serve the sorbet on a hot night, scoop it into chilled bowls and serve or, if you have room in the refrigerator, refreeze the sorbet in the serving bowls.

LIQUID SUGGESTIONS
A sparkling white is always a good way to start an evening outside. At the end of the day, some people may appreciate a good cold beer. Both the prawns and the salmon would be good with a chenin blanc or a sauvignon blanc. The sorbet can be served with a little extra tequila, or serve coffee and a liqueur after the sorbet.

portable food

basics

To ensure that your food reaches your destination in the best possible condition, you will need to put some thought into containers. If, for instance, you have baked frittatas in muffin tins, it is best to transport the frittatas in the tin, wrapping a clean towel around the tin and tying the ends in a knot for a handle. Ask your grandmother if she still has a cake tin with a tight-fitting lid. They're very handy!

utensils

Depending on the type of portable event you are planning or attending, you may wish to take glassware, plates and other breakables. Be sure that you wrap them individually in the napkins you are taking with you. Place cutlery in cutlery rolls to keep everything together.

containers with lids

Be sure you have the right container for the job. Some container lids seal but are not watertight. This could be a disaster if you are carrying food with a dressing or sauce. To test whether your container is watertight, half fill it with water. Place the lid on your container and, over the sink, turn it upside down and sideways, and generally give it a good shake. If the water doesn't leak out, you know your food will be safe.

chillers

Also known as eskies, these are great if you are going out on a hot day. Fill them with ice or freezer blocks, and stack them with drinks, salads, meat and cheeses. If you want to cut down on baggage, a chiller is a good place to fit plates or serving ware. Glassware can be stacked in the chiller if you are using cubed ice.

picnic baskets

These can often be hard to carry when they are full and heavy. You may want to take a basket with two handles, so that the load is shared. Baskets are great for carrying glasses, plates and cutlery.

rugs and chairs

Take one more rug than you think will be necessary because it is always nice to spread out. Remove contents from baskets and turn them upside down for a table for the food, or use the top of your chiller. Fold-up chairs are often bulky, heavy and hard to carry; squatters' chairs are a better alternative.

flasks and hip flasks

Vacuum flasks are a great way to carry warm or cold drinks. Be sure to warm or cool the flask before pouring in the liquid. Hip flasks are small and discreet, handy for carrying a dash of something to add to the champagne or fruit cordial.

containers

chiller

flasks

picnic box

chair and cushions

limeade & spiked passionfruit cordial

thai leaves and chicken baguettes & fresh corn cakes

limeade

1½ cups (12 fl oz) lime juice
¾ cup sugar
crushed ice
soda or mineral water
2 limes, sliced

Place lime juice and sugar in a jug and stir until sugar has dissolved. Chill. When ready to serve, place lime mixture in an ice-filled glass and top with soda or mineral water and lime slices. Serves 6 to 8.

spiked passionfruit cordial

1½ cups (12 fl oz) orange juice, strained
1½ cups (12 fl oz) water
1 cup sugar
1 cup (8 fl oz) passionfruit pulp
½–¾ cup (4–6 fl oz) vodka or gin

Place orange juice, water and sugar in a saucepan over medium heat and stir until sugar has dissolved. Bring mixture to the boil, simmer for 3 minutes, add passionfruit pulp and allow to cool. Add alcohol and store in sterilised bottles in the refrigerator. Serve cordial with soda water or champagne. Serves 6 to 8.

antipasto picnic bread

1 large round loaf crusty bread
filling
3 onions, sliced
2 tablespoons olive oil
12 slices char-grilled marinated eggplant (aubergine)
½ cup mint leaves
20 slices char-grilled marinated zucchini (courgette)
1 cup rocket (arugula) leaves
20 oven-roasted tomato halves
½ cup basil leaves
250g (8 oz) goats' cheese or fresh ricotta
20 slices char-grilled capsicum (pepper) pieces

Cut the top from the bread and scoop out the soft insides leaving a 4cm (1½ inch) thick crust. Place onions and oil in a frypan over medium heat and cook for 6 minutes or until onions are well browned.
To layer bread, place half the onions, eggplant (aubergine), mint, zucchini (courgette), rocket (arugula), tomatoes, basil, cheese and capsicum (pepper) inside the bread cavity in layers. Repeat layers and replace top of bread. Wrap loaf in a cloth to transport and cut into wedges to serve. Serves 8.

fresh corn cakes

3 cobs corn, husks and silk removed
550g (17¾ oz) pumpkin, peeled and chopped
½ cup couscous
½ cup (4 fl oz) boiling water
¼ teaspoon ground cumin
1 red chilli, seeded and chopped
sea salt and pepper
flour to coat

Place corn and pumpkin in a large saucepan of boiling water and cook for 5–8 minutes or until both are soft. Drain and mash pumpkin. Remove corn kernels from cobs. Place couscous in a bowl and pour over boiling water. Allow couscous to stand for 5 minutes or until it is tender. Combine couscous, corn, pumpkin, cumin, chilli, and salt and pepper to taste.
With wet hands, shape mixture into small patties. Toss patties lightly in flour. To cook patties, heat 2cm (¾ inch) of oil in a frypan over high heat. Add patties to pan and cook for 2 minutes on each side or until they are golden and crisp. Serve warm or cold with a spicy chutney. Makes 25.

thai leaves and chicken baguettes

1 baguette, cut into 4
filling
2 tablespoons lemon juice
2 teaspoons sesame oil
2 red chillies, seeded and chopped
2 tablespoons soy sauce
2 chicken breast fillets, thickly sliced
⅓ cup Thai basil leaves
⅓ cup coriander leaves
⅓ cup mint leaves
12 garlic chives, halved

To make filling, place lemon juice, sesame oil, chillies and soy sauce in a bowl and mix to combine. Add chicken and toss to coat. Allow chicken to marinate for 30 minutes. Combine basil, coriander, mint and chives. Place the herbs in each baguette piece.
Preheat a char grill, barbecue or frypan over high heat. Remove chicken from marinade, place on grill and cook for 2 minutes on each side or until it is cooked through. Pile chicken onto herbs in baguettes and wrap to serve. Serves 4.

antipasto picnic bread

little sweet potato and sage frittatas

eggplant and potato tarts

signature beef pies

blueberry fig tart

eggplant and potato tarts

315g (10 oz) prepared puff pastry
topping
2 eggplants (aubergines), sliced
olive oil
1 tablespoon olive oil, extra
3 potatoes, peeled and thinly sliced
3 brown onions, sliced
2 tablespoons lemon thyme leaves
3 cloves garlic, sliced
sea salt and cracked black pepper
olive oil

Roll out pastry on a lightly floured surface until it is 3mm (1/4 inch) thick. Cut pastry into six 12cm (4¾ inch) circles and place them on lined baking trays.
To make topping, brush eggplant (aubergine) slices lightly with oil and cook in a hot preheated frypan for 2 minutes on each side or until they are golden. Remove eggplant (aubergine) from pan and set aside. Heat extra oil in pan, add potato slices, cook for 2 minutes on each side or until they are golden, and remove from pan. Place onions and lemon thyme in pan and cook over medium heat for 8–10 minutes or until onions are golden and soft, then cool. Spread pastry circles with onion mixture and top with eggplant (aubergine), potato, garlic, and salt and pepper. Drizzle tarts with a little olive oil and bake in a preheated 200°C (400°F) oven for 20–25 minutes or until pastry is golden and topping is cooked. Serves 6.

signature beef pies

500g (1 lb) prepared puff pastry
1 egg, lightly beaten
filling
1 tablespoon oil
2 onions, chopped
500g (1 lb) diced chuck steak
1 cup (8 fl oz) beef stock*
1/3 cup (2¾ fl oz) red wine
2 tablespoons Worcestershire sauce
2 tablespoons tomato paste
2 tablespoons plain (all-purpose) flour
4 tablespoons water
salt and cracked pepper to taste

To make filling, heat oil in a saucepan over high heat. Add onions and cook for 3 minutes or until onions are soft. Add steak to pan and cook for 4 minutes or until meat is sealed. Add stock, wine, Worcestershire sauce and tomato paste. Reduce heat and simmer, uncovered, for 50 minutes or until meat is tender. Combine flour and water into a paste and stir into meat mixture. Bring mixture to the boil and stir for 1 minute. Season to taste with salt and pepper, and allow to cool.
Roll out pastry on a lightly floured surface until it is 2mm (1/8 inch) thick. Cut pastry to fit bases and sides of 6 small pie tins. Place filling in pastry bases and top with pastry circles and press with a fork to seal.
From pastry scraps, cut out names, letters or numbers. Brush pie tops with egg and place pies in a preheated 200°C (400°F) oven. Bake for 15–20 minutes or until pastry is puffed and golden. Makes 6.

little sweet potato and sage frittatas

500g (1 lb) sweet potato, peeled and diced
olive oil
sea salt
4 eggs, lightly beaten
1 cup (8 fl oz) cream
cracked black pepper
1/3 cup grated parmesan cheese
1/4 cup small sage leaves

Place sweet potato, oil and salt in a baking dish and toss to combine. Bake in a preheated 200°C (400°F) oven for 25 minutes or until sweet potato is soft.
Combine eggs, cream, pepper and parmesan, and whisk to combine. Pour mixture into 12 greased shallow patty tins. Sprinkle mixture with roasted sweet potato and sage leaves. Bake frittatas at 160°C (315°F) for 20 minutes or until they are golden and firm to touch. Serve warm or cold with a spicy relish. Makes 12.

blueberry fig tart

1 quantity (350g or 12 oz) sweet shortcrust pastry*
8 fresh figs
250g (8 oz) blueberries
filling
250g (8 oz) butter, softened
1 cup caster (superfine) sugar
250g (8 oz) almond meal
4 eggs
1/2 cup plain (all-purpose) flour
2 teaspoons finely grated lemon rind

Roll out pastry on a lightly floured surface until it is 2mm (1/8 inch) thick. Place pastry in a deep 23 cm (9 inch) tart tin. Prick holes in pastry base and refrigerate for 30 minutes. Line pastry with non-stick baking paper and fill with baking weights or rice. Bake in a preheated 200°C (400°F) oven for 5 minutes. Remove weights or rice and paper, and bake for a further 5 minutes or until pastry is a light golden colour.
To make filling, place butter and sugar in a bowl and beat until light and creamy. Add almond meal, eggs, flour and lemon rind to bowl and mix and until combined.
Spread this mixture over base of pastry. Cut 2 slits through the stems in the tops of the figs. Press figs into almond meal mixture in tin and sprinkle with blueberries.
Bake tart in a preheated 180°C (350°F) oven for 20–30 minutes or until filling is firm and figs are soft. Serve warm or cold with clotted cream. Serves 8 to 10.

coconut cake with mint syrup

125g (4 oz) butter
2 teaspoons grated lemon rind
1 cup caster (superfine) sugar
3 eggs
2 cups desiccated coconut
1 cup self-raising (self-rising) flour
1/3 cup sour cream
mint syrup
1 cup sugar
2 tablespoons lemon juice
3/4 cup (6 fl oz) water
1/2 cup mint leaves

Place butter, lemon rind and sugar in the bowl of an electric mixer and beat until mixture is light and creamy. Add eggs, one at a time, and beat well. Fold through coconut, flour and sour cream, and mix until combined.
Spoon mixture into a lined 20cm (8 inch) round cake tin and bake in a preheated 160°C (315°F) oven for 45 minutes or until cake is cooked when tested with a skewer.
To make mint syrup, place sugar, lemon juice, water and mint in a saucepan over low heat and stir until sugar has dissolved. Allow syrup to simmer for 3 minutes, then strain. Pour hot syrup over hot cake. Keep cake in tin and cover with a lid to transport. Serve cake in wedges with clotted cream. Serves 8 to 10.

double choc brownies

240g (7 1/2 oz) butter
240g (7 1/2 oz) dark chocolate
3 eggs
1 1/2 cups caster (superfine) sugar
1 1/2 cups plain (all-purpose) flour
1/2 cup self-raising (self-rising) flour
1 1/2 cups roughly chopped white chocolate

Place butter and dark chocolate in a saucepan over very low heat and stir until smooth.
Place eggs and caster (superfine) sugar in a bowl and beat until mixture is light and thick. Fold egg mixture through dark chocolate mixture, sifted flours and white chocolate, and pour into a greased and lined 23cm (9 inch) square cake tin. Bake in a preheated 180°C (350°F) oven for 30 minutes or until brownies are set.
Allow brownies to cool, cut into squares and dust with icing sugar or good-quality cocoa. Makes 24 squares.

coconut cake with mint syrup

double choc brownies

menu ideas

picnic at the polo for 8

fresh corn cakes
little sweet potato and sage frittatas
eggplant (aubergine) and potato tarts
blueberry fig tart

FOOD PREP
Start with fresh corn cakes and a spicy chutney, and the little sweet potato and sage frittatas. Serve the eggplant (aubergine) and potato tarts (x 1½) for mains with a salad of mixed green leaves dressed with balsamic vinegar and olive oil. The blueberry fig tart makes a wonderful late-afternoon dessert with coffee and tea. Prepare recipes the day before, and do the cooking and the baking the morning of the picnic.

LIQUID SUGGESTIONS
Start the day with a crisp, sparkling white wine and some spiked passionfruit cordial. Move on to a grassy sauvignon blanc with the nibbles and a lightly wooded chardonnay with the tarts. If the afternoon gets chilly, dispense a little cognac or brandy from a hip flask to accompany the blueberry fig tart.

picnic by the lake for 6

little sweet potato and sage frittatas
antipasto picnic bread
double choc brownies
limeade

FOOD PREP
Try a wrapped box of little sweet potato and sage frittatas for starters followed by the king of the picnic, the antipasto picnic bread, cut into chunky wedges and served with limeade. Prepare recipes the day before, and do the cooking and the baking the morning of the picnic. Finish with sweet, rich double choc brownies, which can be made 2 days in advance and stored in an airtight container.

LIQUID SUGGESTIONS
Take an esky (chiller) full of ice and place it in the shade under a tree. Fill it with limeade and sparkling mineral water, a lightly wooded chardonnay and a bottle of smooth merlot to sip the afternoon away. Have a thermos of hot coffee to serve with the brownies.

picnic at the races for 8

eggplant (aubergine) and potato tarts
Thai leaves and chicken baguettes
coconut cake with mint syrup

FOOD PREP
Cut the eggplant (aubergine) and potato tarts into small pieces to nibble with drinks. Serve the Thai leaves and chicken baguettes (x 2) wrapped in napkins for lunch and later in the afternoon serve coconut cake with mint syrup, which can be made 1 day in advance and stored in an airtight container. Prepare other recipes the day before, and do the cooking and the baking the morning of the picnic.

LIQUID SUGGESTIONS
When you think races, you think bubbly whites and celebrations. You may choose to drink sparkling white all day long. The spicy baguettes would also be great with a dry riesling. All those bubbles can make you a little weary, so a quick short black with some sweet coconut cake will pick you back up.

drinks

basics

For a successful drinks party, make sure you have all the bar accessories and drink-making supplies in order before the guests arrive. When serving tricky morsels, be sure your guests have a place to put their prawn tails and scallop shells. Otherwise, you'll be finding abandoned debris in your pot plants for months to come.

ice

You can never have too much ice at a drinks party. Fill large buckets with cubed ice to chill champagne, wine and mixers at least 1 hour before guests arrive. Have plenty of ice at the bar for cocktails. Set a block of ice on a tray with an icepick for large, cooling shards of ice for drinks.

corkscrew

The old-fashioned and extremely reliable waiter's friend corkscrew is a must. Plain stainless steel will serve you well for years. If you are planning to have many guests, make sure you have a few corkscrews. If you misplace your only one, there will be no party!

blender

If you want to make drinks with lots of crushed ice, make sure you have a blender with a little power behind it. You won't necessarily need a commercial blender, but a glass jug and good 400-watt-or-above motor will do the job well.

cocktail shaker

Almost every home bar seems to have a cocktail shaker on a shelf collecting dust. What you may have thought was a token bar element is an essential item. Be aware that cocktail shakers range in price.

ice crusher

If you are going to serve drinks over crushed ice, you may need to invest in an ice crusher. Manual ones are fairly inexpensive, or you can go for the fully electrified version.

glasses

Make sure you have plenty of glasses and hire extras if you need to. Glasses don't have to strictly match the cocktail, but a small range is good: large glasses for icy fruit daiquiris and frozen margaritas and smaller glasses for the more potent berry martini.

swizzle sticks and bits

Search for fun swizzle sticks, straws and drink accessories. Remember, they can never be too tacky.

ice crusher

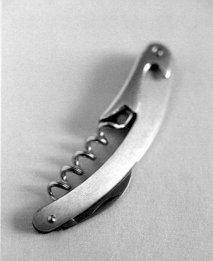

corkscrew

cocktail shaker

blender

straws and swizzle sticks

lime and ginger grilled scallops

vanilla vodka

lime and ginger scallops

24 scallops in half shell
lime and ginger butter
2 tablespoons very finely shredded ginger
2 teaspoons finely grated lime rind
2 teaspoons sesame oil
cracked black pepper
2 tablespoons lemon thyme leaves
100g (3½ oz) butter, softened slightly

To make lime and ginger butter, place ginger, lime rind, sesame oil, pepper, thyme and butter in a bowl and mix to combine. Spread a little of the seasoned butter over each scallop. Before serving, place scallops under a preheated very hot grill and cook for 1 minute or until they are golden. Be careful not to overcook the scallops as the shell heats up and continues cooking them even after they are removed from the grill. Serve immediately. Makes 24.

vanilla vodka

750ml (24 fl oz) vodka
3 vanilla beans,* split

Place vanilla beans in vodka and allow to infuse on a window sill for at least 1 week before serving. To serve straight, freeze vodka with vanilla beans for 24 hours prior to serving. Serve vanilla vodka over ice with tonic or soda. Makes 750ml (24 fl oz).

campari and ruby grapefruit

500ml (16 fl oz) bottled ruby grapefruit juice
⅓ cup (2¾ fl oz) Campari
6 mint sprigs
315ml (10 fl oz) tonic or soda water
ice

Place grapefruit juice, Campari, mint and tonic or soda in a jug and stir to combine. Pour drink into chilled glasses filled with ice and serve. Serves 3 to 4.

iced berry martini

½ cup (4 fl oz) gin
⅓ cup (2¾ fl oz) sweet vermouth
8 ice cubes
4 tablespoons puréed berries

Place gin, vermouth, ice and berry purée in a cocktail shaker. Shake well and strain into a well-chilled glass. Serves 2.

seared and marinated tuna

500g (1 lb) piece sashimi tuna
2 teaspoons sesame oil
2 teaspoons ginger, minced
4 tablespoons soy sauce
2 tablespoons mirin
2 tablespoons lemon juice
1 tablespoon finely chopped flat-leaf (Italian) parsley
1 quantity sushi rice*
3 sheets toasted nori*
pickled ginger

Brush tuna with sesame oil. Heat a frypan over high heat. Place tuna in frypan and cook for 5 seconds on each side, and set aside. Combine ginger, soy sauce, mirin, lemon juice and parsley in a shallow dish. Place tuna in marinade and refrigerate, turning tuna occasionally, for 1–2 hours. To serve, remove tuna from marinade and slice thinly.
Place half the rice on a piece of non-stick baking paper and place paper on a sushi rolling mat. Roll rice in paper and mat until it is a firm cylinder. With a serrated knife, cut rice into discs 2cm (¾ inch) thick. Repeat with remaining rice. Cut nori into squares bigger than the rice discs and place squares on a serving platter.
Before serving, top nori with rice disc, a piece of pickled ginger and a slice of tuna. Spoon over a little of the marinade and serve. Makes 32 pieces.

pimm's citrus crush

⅓ cup (2¾ fl oz) freshly crushed lemon juice
⅓ cup (2¾ fl oz) freshly crushed lime juice
⅓ cup (2¾ fl oz) freshly crushed orange juice
⅓ cup (2¾ fl oz) freshly crushed ruby grapefruit juice
1 tablespoon caster (superfine) sugar
500ml (16 fl oz) tonic water
½ cup (4 fl oz) Pimm's no. 1

Place lemon, lime, orange and ruby grapefruit juices in a jug. Add sugar and stir to dissolve. Add tonic and Pimm's, and serve over ice. Serves 4 to 6.

classic champagne framboise

750ml (24 fl oz) bottle champagne
10 tablespoons framboise* or raspberry liqueur
fresh raspberries

Place champagne on ice 1 hour before serving. Pour 2 tablespoons of framboise into each of 5 glasses. Top with champagne and raspberries. Serves 5.

seared and marinated tuna

iced berry martini & classic champagne framboise

campari and ruby grapefruit & pimm's citrus crush

balsamic fig bruschetta

frozen vodka slushie

white lime

balsamic fig bruschetta

1 tablespoon butter
1/4 cup (2 fl oz) balsamic vinegar
2 teaspoons sugar
6 figs, cut into quarters
filling
250g (8 oz) blue cheese (with bite and body)
1/3 cup (135g or 41/2 oz) mascarpone^
1 tablespoon roughly chopped flat-leaf (Italian) parsley
cracked black pepper
bruschetta
24 thin slices sourdough baguette
olive oil
3 cloves garlic, halved

To make filling, combine blue cheese, mascarpone, parsley and pepper to taste. Heat butter, balsamic vinegar and sugar in a frypan over high heat. Stir and allow to simmer until mixture has thickened slightly. Place fig quarters in pan, a few at a time, cook for 30 seconds on each side or until they are lightly coated, and set aside.
To make bruschetta, brush baguette slices with olive oil. Place slices under a hot grill and cook until bread is golden on both sides. When cooked, rub bread with garlic halves for flavour.
To serve, place a small amount of blue cheese mixture on each slice of bread and top with a fig. Warm bruschetta under a low grill before serving. Makes 24.

salmon and pickled cucumber

300g (10 oz) piece sashimi salmon
24 triangles of Lebanese or flatbread
pickled cucumbers
2 Lebanese cucumbers, thinly sliced
sea salt
1/4 cup (2 fl oz) white wine vinegar
1 tablespoon chopped dill
2 teaspoons caster (superfine) sugar
1–2 teaspoons wasabi* paste
cracked black pepper

To make pickled cucumbers, place cucumber slices in a colander and sprinkle with sea salt. Allow cucumbers to drain for 15 minutes. Wash and pat dry slices with absorbent paper. Place cucumbers in a bowl, and pour over combined vinegar, dill, sugar, wasabi and pepper. Allow cucumbers to marinate for 30 minutes.
To serve, cut salmon into 24 slices. Place a piece of salmon to one side of the bread. Drain vinegar from cucumbers and place a small pile of cucumber slices on top of the salmon. Make a slit in the side of each bread triangle and thread the corner through the opposite corner or secure bread with a toothpick and serve. Makes 24 pieces.

frozen vodka slushie

1 cup sugar
4 cups (32 fl oz) boiling water
11/2 cups (12 fl oz) lemon or lime juice
1/2 –3/4 cup (4–6 fl oz) vodka

Place sugar and boiling water in a bowl and stir until sugar has dissolved. Cool mixture slightly before adding lemon or lime juice and vodka. Place slushie mixture in freezer for 2 hours and then stir with a fork. Freeze for another 2 hours or until slushie is firm. Break ice with a fork or blend until smooth and serve immediately. Serves 4.

white lime

750ml (24 fl oz) white spirit, such as vodka, gin or white rum
4 limes, sliced

Place white spirit and limes in a clean bottle and refrigerate. Allow limes to infuse into spirit for at least 4 days before serving over ice, with soda or tonic. To serve straight, place limes and spirit in freezer for a few hours. Makes 750ml (12 fl oz).

kaffir chicken on betel leaves

2 teaspoons sesame oil
1 tablespoon finely shredded ginger
1 stalk lemongrass,* finely chopped
6 kaffir lime* leaves, shredded
3 red chillies, seeded and chopped
300g (10 oz) minced chicken breast
2 tablespoons lemon juice
1 tablespoon fish sauce
2 tablespoons soy sauce
12–18 betel leaves* or baby English spinach leaves to serve
coriander sprigs and sliced chilli to serve

Place sesame oil in a frypan or wok over high heat. Add ginger, lemongrass, lime leaves and chillies to pan and cook for 1 minute. Add chicken to pan and cook for 4 minutes or until chicken is cooked. Stir through lemon juice, fish sauce and soy sauce, and cook for 1 minute. Wash betel or spinach leaves and dry on absorbent paper. Place piles of warm chicken filling on each leaf and serve immediately with a sprig of coriander and sliced chilli. Makes 12 to 18 pieces.

kaffir chicken on betel leaves

sesame and soy pumpkin

1/2 small, sweet pumpkin
oil
sea salt
3 tablespoons honey
2 teaspoons sesame oil
1 tablespoon sesame seeds
1 tablespoon finely chopped ginger
3 tablespoons soy sauce
2 tablespoons Chinese cooking (shao hsing) wine or sherry

Peel pumpkin, cut it into bite-sized pieces and toss in oil and salt. Place in a single layer on a baking dish and bake in a preheated 200°C (400°F) oven for 25 minutes or until they are tender.
In a large frypan, combine honey, sesame oil, sesame seeds, ginger, soy sauce and wine. Allow mixture to simmer until it is quite syrupy. Add pumpkin to frypan, a few pieces at a time, and toss to coat. Remove pumpkin from pan and place pieces on a baking tray lined with non-stick baking paper. Return pumpkin to oven and bake at 150°C (300°F) for 5 minutes. Serve warm with toothpicks. Makes 24 pieces.

chilli and lemon olives

500g (1 lb) firm kalamata olives
3 cloves garlic, unpeeled
2 red chillies, chopped
3 tablespoons lemon juice
1 tablespoon shredded lemon rind
1 tablespoon rosemary leaves
3 tablespoons olive oil

Before marinating olives, test them for saltiness. If the olives are salty, place them in a large bowl of cold water. Drain olives and place them in fresh water every 30 minutes until they are no longer overly salty.
Place garlic in a dry frypan over high heat and toast on all sides until it is well browned. Remove garlic from skin and mash. Add chillies, lemon juice and rind, rosemary and oil to garlic, and mix to combine. Pour marinade over olives and refrigerate for at least 8 hours before serving. Olives are best marinated for 2–3 days before serving. Serves 6 to 8.

duck liver pâté

550g (1 lb 1³/4 oz) duck livers
1/2 cup (4 fl oz) cognac
2 tablespoons butter
1 teaspoon tarragon leaves
1/4 teaspoon grated nutmeg
cracked black pepper
75g (2¹/2 oz) butter, chopped

Remove any discoloured or tough white pieces of liver. Place livers in a bowl with cognac and refrigerate for 2 hours. Heat butter in a large frypan over high heat until it is bubbling. Drain livers from cognac, reserve cognac and add livers to pan. Toss livers in butter until they change colour, then remove from pan. Add cognac, tarragon, nutmeg and pepper to pan and cook for 2–3 minutes or until liquid is reduced to a third. Place livers and cognac mixture in a food processor and process until smooth. Press liver mixture through a fine sieve and return to cleaned food processor. Add extra butter to liver mixture and process until it is smooth. Cover pâté with plastic wrap and refrigerate for 2–3 hours or until it is firm. Serve pâté on toasted slices of bagel with pepper pears. Serves 12.

pepper pears

3 tablespoons apple cider vinegar
2 tablespoons balsamic vinegar
2 tablespoons sugar
cracked black pepper
2 firm pears, peeled and thinly sliced

Place cider vinegar, balsamic vinegar, sugar and pepper in a frypan over low heat and stir until sugar dissolves. Add pears to pan and allow to simmer for 1 minute. Remove pan from heat and allow pears to stand for 1 hour before serving them at room temperature with pâté. Serves 12.

peach julep

1 cup (8 fl oz) water
1/2 cup sugar
1¹/2 cups mint leaves
1¹/2 cups (12 fl oz) fresh white peach juice
1/2–³/4 cup (4–6 fl oz) bourbon or brandy
soda

Place water and sugar in a saucepan over low heat and stir until sugar has dissolved. Add mint leaves to pan and simmer for 3 minutes. Remove pan from heat and allow to stand for 30 minutes, then strain syrup. Add sugar syrup to chilled peach juice and bourbon, and mix to combine. Chill julep, serve over crushed ice and top with soda. Serves 6.

sesame and soy pumpkin

chilli and lemon olives

salmon and pickled cucumber

duck liver pâté with pepper pears

peach julep

menu ideas

pre-dinner drinks for 8

balsamic fig bruschetta
sesame and soy pumpkin
lime and ginger scallops
Pimm's citrus crush
classic champagne framboise*

FOOD PREP

As a prelude to dining and to awaken the tastebuds, start with the balsamic fig bruschetta, followed by the sesame and soy pumpkin, and the lime and ginger grilled scallops. If there is enough food with the drinks, you can go straight into mains for dinner followed by dessert and cheese. The balsamic fig bruschetta and the pumpkin can be made ahead of time and gently warmed before serving. Prepare the lime and ginger butter for the scallops beforehand and grill scallops just before serving.

LIQUID SUGGESTIONS

Start with something light and refreshing such as the Pimm's citrus crush or the classic champagne framboise.* Serve a rich pinot noir, a mellow cabernet sauvignon or an aged chardonnay to complement the food.

celebration drinks party for 10

lime and ginger scallops
chilli and lemon olives
duck liver pâté
pepper pears
balsamic fig bruschetta
classic champagne framboise*

FOOD PREP

When your guests arrive, serve the lime and ginger scallops as a tastebud starter. Follow the scallops with small cups or beakers of the chilli and lemon olives served with small olive forks. The duck liver pâté with pepper pears and the balsamic fig bruschetta will make a substantial finish. You can make the pâté and pears prior to the party and marinate the olives the day before.

LIQUID SUGGESTIONS

When guests arrive, serve a classic champagne framboise* (x 2), straight bubbly or a light pinot noir. To carry them through the evening, keep serving the bubbly and maybe add a smooth cabernet sauvignon to complement the rich pâté and bruschetta.

cocktails for 6

sesame and soy pumpkin
seared and marinated tuna
kaffir chicken on betel leaves
frozen vodka slushie
campari and ruby grapefruit
vanilla vodka

FOOD PREP

Start with the sesame and soy pumpkin, and the seared and marinated tuna. After these, the kaffir chicken on betel leaves will fill stomachs nicely. All recipes can be prepared beforehand. Warm the pumpkin and the chicken topping for the leaves before serving.

LIQUID SUGGESTIONS

Start off strong with frozen vodka slushies (x 3), moving on to campari and ruby grapefruit. A good, well-flavoured cold beer is also great if it is a hot summer night, so fill a large tub with ice. Serve vanilla vodka over ready-made fruit sorbet to finish.

in a flash

basics

oils and vinegars

A splash of oil or vinegar here or there could be the flavour saviour in a quickly thrown-together meal. Be sure to buy oils and vinegars of good quality. Like many things, you pay for what you get. Store oils and vinegars in a cool, dark place.

OLIVE OIL Have a light olive oil as well as a good, extra virgin, deep green, fruity one on hand for varying intensities of flavour.

SESAME OIL Buy a good-quality Asian sesame oil and use it sparingly as it may overpower other flavours.

CHILLI OIL The strength of the heat varies from extreme to mild, so test before splashing chilli oil into a dish. It is a great way to add chilli flavour in a hurry.

VEGETABLE OIL This oil is good for frying and when you wish to use a mild oil in dressings and so on.

HERB OILS These are great in dressings or as a base for a well-flavoured dish.

WHITE WINE AND RED WINE VINEGAR Purchase good-quality wine vinegars for the best flavours.

BALSAMIC VINEGAR Balsamic vinegar is aged in a similar way to wine and, like wine, good quality is a must.

HERB VINEGAR This vinegar makes a great base for a fast salad dressing. It's easy to make your own.

sauces, pastes and preserves

For great flavour bases for quick and tasty marinades, dressings or additions to salads or pastas, keep a good selection of sauces and condiments in the cupboard. Check their labels, as some need to be refrigerated after opening.

SOY SAUCE, OYSTER SAUCE, CHILLI SAUCE, FISH SAUCE Keep a good variety of these sauces handy for marinades, dipping sauces, curries, stir fries and much more (see p. 32).

PEPPER AND SEA SALT Use peppercorns in a grinder for freshly cracked pepper. When using sea salt, grind the rock form or crush the flaked variety in your fingertips before adding to food.

DRIED CHILLIES, SEEDS AND HERBS Purchase these in small amounts as their flavour dulls over time. Store dried chillies, seeds and herbs in airtight containers. Grind whole spices as required.

WASABI This is an addictive green horseradish paste. It's a must-have for sushi or marinades. You can buy it in paste or powdered form. (I prefer the Japanese paste form.)

MUSTARDS AND CHUTNEYS These can save a sandwich, a marinade, a dressing and much more. Keep a good variety at close range. I keep onion marmalade; seeded, Dijon and honey mustards; chilli jam; mango and lemongrass chutneys; and whatever else has a bit of spice or kick.

OLIVES AND CAPERS Keep these in jars in the cupboard or refrigerator. They are great to add to salads, sandwiches, pastas and so on for a little saltiness and zing.

store cupboard essentials

Keep a good selection of dry goods in your store cupboard so you have the basic building blocks to create a great meal at short notice.

LONG-LIFE STOCK PACKS The quality of these varies, so test them out. In a perfect world we would have time to make our own stock. Good-quality frozen stock is available at some stores.

DRIED PASTA AND NOODLES These solve many a 'nothing for dinner' dilemma. Keep a good variety in the cupboard as standbys.

JASMINE RICE, ARBORIO RICE AND SHORT-GRAIN RICE These are essential accompaniments for quick stir fries or curries. My favourite, arborio, takes a little longer to prepare, but it's therapeutic to sit on a stool sipping a glass of wine while stirring risotto.

POLENTA It's extremely rewarding on a chilly night to sit down to some soft polenta with fried herbs, blue cheese and pepper.

LENTILS From red to green to brown, lentils make a great base for salads, soups and curries.

COUSCOUS Cover couscous with boiling stock, toss through a little butter, pepper and herbs, and hey presto. How did we live without it?

COOKING WINES A dry red and a dry white wine, and a bottle of mirin will fit the bill. Don't buy really cheap wine as the flavour will come through in your cooking.

balsamic vinegar

herb oil and chilli oil

vegetable oil, olive oil and sesame oil

red and white wine vinegars

herb vinegar

119

mustards and chutneys   dried spices and chillies

salt and pepper   preserved goods

pastes

red and white cooking wines

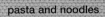
pasta and noodles

stock

rice

lentils and grains

roast fennel and olive salad

rocket and parmesan flatbread salad

roast fennel and olive salad

4 baby fennel bulbs, quartered
2 red onions, cut into eight pieces
4 Roma (egg) tomatoes, halved
3 tablespoons olive oil
2 tablespoons oregano leaves
beet leaves or salad greens
1 cup Ligurian or small olives
dressing
3 tablespoons apple cider vinegar
2 teaspoons Dijon mustard
2 tablespoons olive oil
1 clove garlic, crushed

Place fennel, onions and tomatoes in a baking dish. Heat oil in a small saucepan over low heat. Add oregano to pan and heat for 3 minutes. Pour oil over vegetables and bake in a preheated 200°C (400°F) oven for 30 minutes.
To make dressing, whisk together vinegar, mustard, oil and garlic. To serve, place vegetables on a bed of baby beet or salad greens on serving plates. Sprinkle salad with olives and dressing. Serves 4 as a starter, or serve with grilled meats or fish as a main meal.

mint couscous with fried tomatoes

1½ cups couscous
1¾ cups (14 fl oz) boiling vegetable* or chicken stock*
1 tablespoon olive oil
4 ripe tomatoes, thickly sliced
cracked black pepper
2 teaspoons oil, extra
1 onion, chopped
2 tablespoons baby capers
1 tablespoon grated lemon rind
¼ cup roughly chopped blanched almonds
3 tablespoons chopped mint
2 bunches (100g or 3½ oz) rocket (arugula) leaves
175g (6 oz) marinated feta cheese, sliced

Place couscous in a bowl and pour over boiling stock. Allow to stand for 5 minutes or until stock has been absorbed. Heat oil in a large frypan over medium heat. Sprinkle tomato slices with pepper and place them in pan. Cook tomatoes for 4–5 minutes on each side or until they are well browned. Heat extra oil in a separate frypan over high heat. Add onion and cook for 3 minutes or until it is soft. Add capers, lemon rind and almonds to pan and cook for 2 minutes. Add couscous and mint to pan and cook for 2 minutes or until mixture is heated. Place couscous on serving plates, top with rocket (arugula), cheese and fried tomatoes. Serves 6 as a starter or 4 as a main meal.

rocket and parmesan flatbread salad

2 bunches (200g or 7 oz) rocket (arugula)
3 tablespoons balsamic vinegar
2 ruby grapefruit, peeled and segmented
½–¾ cup shaved parmesan cheese
cracked black pepper
parmesan flatbread
2 flat lavash breads
⅓ cup finely grated parmesan cheese, extra
¼ cup (2 fl oz) olive oil

Combine rocket (arugula), balsamic vinegar, grapefruit, parmesan shavings and pepper in a bowl.
To make parmesan flatbread, cut lavash into 16 equal pieces. Combine extra parmesan and oil, and brush over one side of bread strips. Place bread strips under a preheated hot grill and cook for 1 minute or until they are golden. Turn bread, brush with parmesan mixture and grill for 1 minute or until they are golden.
Cross 4 bread strips on each serving plate. Top with rocket (arugula) and serve.
Serves 4 as a starter or serve salad with char-grilled meat or fish as a main meal.

noodle bowl with barbecue pork

8 dried Chinese mushrooms
400g (13 oz) fresh udon* or Hokkien noodles
3 cups (24 fl oz) chicken stock*
½ cup (4 fl oz) Chinese cooking (shao hsing) wine or sherry
6 slices ginger
1 green chilli, seeded and sliced
4 shallots, chopped
2 tablespoons coriander leaves
2 cups chopped bok choy or choy sum
350g (12 oz) Chinese barbecue pork* (char sui)

Place mushrooms in a bowl, cover them with boiling water and soak them for 5 minutes or until they are soft. Drain, pat dry and finely slice mushrooms.
Place noodles in hot water for 1 minute, then drain. If you are using dried noodles, place them in a saucepan of boiling water until they are soft, then drain. Divide noodles among serving bowls.
Place stock, wine, ginger, chilli, shallots and coriander in a saucepan over high heat and bring to the boil. Add greens to stock and then pour stock over noodles in bowls. Slice pork, place slices in bowls with noodles and toss to combine. Sprinkle noodles with mushrooms before serving. Serve with chilli sauce or chopped chillies. Serves 6 as a starter or 4 as a main meal.

noodle bowl with barbecue pork

sesame-crusted ocean trout

4 x 180g (6 oz) pieces ocean trout fillet

1/4 cup sesame seeds

1/4 cup black sesame seeds*

1 tablespoon oil

greens

1 bunch gai larn, trimmed and halved

1 bunch choy sum, trimmed and halved

2 teaspoons sesame oil

1 tablespoon shredded ginger

3 tablespoons oyster sauce

2 tablespoons soy sauce

1 tablespoon sugar

3 tablespoons Chinese cooking (shao hsing) wine or sherry

Remove skin and visible bones from trout. Combine sesame seeds and place them in a shallow dish. Press both sides of trout pieces into sesame seeds to form a crust. Place greens in a saucepan of boiling water and cook for 1 minute, then drain.

Heat sesame oil in a pan over high heat. Add ginger and cook for 1 minute. Add oyster and soy sauces, sugar and wine, and simmer for 4 minutes or until thickened.

Place a frypan over low heat. Add oil and place trout in pan. Cook trout over low heat for 1–2 minutes on each side or until it is cooked medium-rare. To serve, toss greens in frypan with the simmering sauce and place on serving plates. Top greens with sesame-crusted trout and serve. Serves 4.

lamb with garlic mash

8 double lamb cutlets, trimmed

1 teaspoon cracked black pepper

3 tablespoons chopped mint

1/2 cup (4 fl oz) red wine

1 tablespoon seeded mustard

1/4 teaspoon ground cumin

garlic mash

6 cloves garlic, unpeeled

6 mashing potatoes, peeled and chopped

2 tablespoons butter

1–1 1/4 cups (8–10 fl oz) hot milk

pinch sea salt

Place lamb cutlets in a shallow dish. Combine pepper, mint, wine, mustard and cumin, and pour over lamb. Allow cutlets to marinate for at least 30 minutes, preferably 2 hours.

To make garlic mash, place unpeeled garlic in a dry frypan over medium heat. Allow to cook, turning occasionally, for 10 minutes or until garlic skins are golden brown, then cool. Squeeze garlic from skins and mash with a fork.

Place potatoes in a saucepan of boiling water and simmer for 6 minutes or until they are tender. While potatoes are cooking, drain marinade from lamb and place marinade in a small saucepan. Allow marinade to simmer over low heat until it is syrupy. Heat a frypan over high heat. Add lamb to pan and cook for 2–3 minutes on each side or until it is cooked to your liking.

To finish mash, drain potatoes, return them to warm pan with butter, and mash with a whisk while slowly adding milk until potatoes are thick and creamy. Stir through salt and mashed garlic.

To serve, place a pile of mash on plates with lamb and spoon over the sauce. Serve with a salad of rocket (arugula) and balsamic vinegar or baby spinach leaves. Serves 4.

jasmine rice pilaf with salt-roasted chicken

4 chicken breast fillets, skin on

olive oil

sea salt

jasmine rice pilaf

1 tablespoon oil

1 tablespoon butter

2 onions, chopped

2 coriander roots

4 kaffir lime* leaves

2 red chillies, seeded and chopped

1 1/2 cups jasmine rice

1 1/2 cups (12 fl oz) vegetable* or chicken stock*

1–1 1/2 cups (8–12 fl oz) water

To cook chicken, rub its skin with olive oil and sea salt, being careful not to salt the flesh. Heat a frypan over high heat. Place chicken in pan, skin side down, and cook for 2 minutes or until it is well browned. Place chicken in a baking dish and bake in a preheated 150° (300°F) oven for 30 minutes.

To make pilaf, heat oil and butter in a heavy-based saucepan over medium heat. Add onions to pan and cook for 3 minutes or until they are soft. Add coriander roots, kaffir lime leaves and chillies, and cook for 1 minute. Add rice to pan and cook for 2 minutes. Add stock and most of the water to pan. Cover pan and simmer over medium-low heat for 15 minutes or until rice is soft and liquid has been absorbed. More water may be added if required. Remove lime leaves and coriander roots.

To serve, place pilaf in bowls on the side of serving plates and place chicken on serving plates. Tomato pickle or spicy mango chutney make a good accompaniment. Serves 4.

mint couscous with fried tomatoes

sesame-crusted ocean trout

127

lamb with garlic mash

jasmine rice pilaf with salt-roasted chicken

linguine with asparagus and baked ricotta   ginger pork with lentils

spaghetti with lemon, chilli, garlic and rocket

750g (1½ lb) fresh spaghetti, linguine or fettuccine
3–4 tablespoons light olive oil
2 cloves garlic, crushed
4 tablespoons baby capers
1½ teaspoons dried chilli flakes or 3 fresh red chillies, seeded and sliced
2 teaspoons finely grated lemon rind
3 tablespoons lemon juice
3–4 cups roughly chopped rocket (arugula) leaves
¾ cup grated parmesan cheese
cracked black pepper

Cook spaghetti in a saucepan of rapidly boiling water until it is al dente.
While pasta is cooking, heat oil in a large saucepan over high heat. Add garlic and capers and sauté for 1 minute. Add chillies, and lemon rind and juice to pan and cook for another minute. Drain pasta and add it to garlic mixture with rocket (arugula) and parmesan. Toss to combine and serve pasta with a generous sprinkling of black pepper and warm, crusty bread. Serves 6 as a starter or 4 (with salad) as a main meal.

linguine with asparagus and baked ricotta

500g (1 lb) dried linguine
2 tablespoons butter
2 tablespoons oil
¾ cup chopped hazelnuts
3 tablespoons sage leaves
2 cloves garlic, crushed
3 tablespoons lemon juice
sea salt and cracked black pepper
3 bunches (600g or 1¼ lb) asparagus, trimmed and blanched
150g (5 oz) baby spinach leaves
300g (10 oz) baked ricotta, sliced
balsamic vinegar

Place linguine in a saucepan of boiling water and cook for 10–12 minutes or until it is al dente.
While linguine is cooking, heat butter and oil in a frypan over high heat. Add hazelnuts and sage to pan, and cook for 2–3 minutes or until nuts are golden. Add garlic to pan and cook for 1 minute. Add lemon juice, salt and pepper, asparagus and drained linguine to pan and toss to combine.
To serve, place spinach leaves on serving plates and top with slices of ricotta. Place linguine on leaves and ricotta, and drizzle with balsamic vinegar. Serves 6 a starter or 4 as a main meal.

ginger pork with lentils

1 tablespoon oil
2 tablespoons shredded ginger
1 tablespoon brown sugar
2 tablespoons lime juice
1 tablespoon balsamic vinegar
750g (1½ lb) pork fillet medallions 3cm (1¼ inches) thick
refried lentils
1½ cups puy lentils
2½ cups (20 fl oz) water
1 tablespoon oil
2 teaspoons cumin seeds
1 tablespoon lime juice
2 tablespoons chopped coriander leaves
sea salt and cracked black pepper

Heat oil in a frypan over high heat. Add ginger to pan and cook for 2 minutes or until it becomes a light golden colour. Add sugar, lime juice and vinegar, and simmer until mixture has thickened, then remove from pan and set aside.
To make refried lentils, place lentils and water in a saucepan and bring to the boil. Reduce heat to simmer. Cover lentils and cook for 5–8 minutes or until all liquid has been absorbed and lentils have softened. Heat oil in a frypan over high heat. Add cumin seeds and cook for 1 minute. Add lentils, lime juice, coriander, salt and pepper, and cook, stirring, for 5 minutes or until lentils are soft and heated through.
To finish pork, heat a frypan over high heat. Add pork medallions and cook for 2–3 minutes on each side or until pork is cooked to your liking, then pour over caramelised ginger and heat for 1 minute. To serve, place lentils on a serving plate, and top with pork and ginger syrup. Serves 4.

spaghetti with lemon, chilli, garlic and rocket

tamarillos soaked in sauternes

6 tamarillos (tree tomatoes)
1 cup (8 fl oz) water
1/2 cup sugar
1 vanilla bean,* halved
250ml (8 fl oz) sauternes or late-harvest riesling

Place tamarillos (tree tamarillos) in a saucepan of boiling water and cook for 1 minute, then drain and peel away skins. Slice tamarillos (tree tomatoes) in half, leaving stalk end intact. Place water, sugar and vanilla bean in a saucepan over low heat and stir until sugar dissolves. Bring syrup to the boil and simmer for 3 minutes. Add tamarillos (tree tomatoes) and sauternes, and remove pan from heat. Allow to soak for at least 1 hour or overnight. Serve tamarillos (tree tomatoes) in deep bowls with thick cream on the side. Serves 6.

autumn plum and strawberry crumbles

3 cups chopped ripe autumn plums
1 cup halved and hulled strawberries
2–3 tablespoons sugar
1/2 teaspoon ground cinnamon
2 tablespoons lemon juice
topping
1/2 cup brown sugar
2/3 cup rolled oats
1/4 cup plain (all-purpose) flour
90g (3 oz) butter, softened
1 teaspoon ground cinnamon, extra

Combine fruit with sugar, cinnamon and lemon juice. Divide mixture between 4 ramekins.
To make topping, combine sugar, oats, flour, butter and extra cinnamon. Pile oat mixture on top of fruit. Place ramekins in a preheated 180°C (350°F) oven and bake for 25 minutes or until topping is golden and crisp, and fruit is soft. Serve crumbles warm or cold with vanilla bean ice cream. Makes 4.

marsala peaches with mascarpone

1/3 cup (2¾ fl oz) marsala
2 tablespoons brown sugar
2 tablespoons orange juice
4 peaches, halved
150g (5 oz) mascarpone*
1½ tablespoons icing (confectioners) sugar
3 tablespoons marsala, extra

Combine marsala, sugar and orange juice, and mix until sugar has dissolved. Pour mixture over peaches and allow them to macerate for 20 minutes.
Combine mascarpone and icing (confectioners) sugar and mix until smooth. Place peaches and marinade in a hot preheated frypan and cook for 2–3 minutes on each side or until peaches are golden.
To serve, place peaches on a serving plate. Place a spoonful of mascarpone next to the peaches and make a small indentation in the mascarpone. Fill indentation with extra marsala. Pour pan juices over peaches and serve. Serves 4.

tamarillos soaked in sauternes

marsala peaches with mascarpone

autumn plum and strawberry crumbles

menu ideas

impromptu dinner for 4

spaghetti with lemon, chilli, garlic and rocket (arugula)
marsala peaches with mascarpone*

FOOD PREP
For mains serve spaghetti with lemon, chilli, garlic and rocket (arugula) with bread. Finish with a really simple dessert of grilled fruit such as marsala peaches with mascarpone.* You can swap the peaches for pears or any other fruit good for grilling. If you are hard pressed finding mascarpone at short notice, serve thick cream or good-quality ready-made ice cream.

LIQUID SUGGESTIONS
Quickly fill glasses with sparkling wine or a lively, refreshing white wine. If you have a few marinated olives in the refrigerator, throw them on a platter. The spicy pasta is best served with a fresh, crisp sauvignon blanc, semillon or blend of these. Top off dessert with a good, sweet, chilled sticky.

school night dinner for 6

rocket (arugula) and parmesan flatbread salad
lamb with garlic mash
tamarillos soaked in sauternes

FOOD PREP
Start with something simple and light such as the rocket (arugula) and parmesan flatbread salad (x 1½). If you have time, make the flatbreads beforehand and store them in an airtight container. For mains, try the lamb cutlets with garlic mash (x 1½) and, if you remember, marinate the cutlets the morning before the dinner. Place a large bowl of steamed spinach with lots of cracked black pepper and lemon juice in the middle of the table. Finish with the tamarillos soaked in sauternes for dessert. Serve the tamarillos chilled in the hotter months and warm in the colder.

LIQUID SUGGESTIONS
The peppery rocket (arugula) salad could stand up to a lightly wooded chardonnay, but I would rather serve it with a sauvignon blanc. The mustard lamb could be matched with a cabernet sauvignon or shiraz. Serve dessert with a sweet dessert wine with strong fruit and honey undertones.

fast dinner for 8

roast fennel and olive salad
jasmine rice pilaf with salt-roasted chicken
tamarillos soaked in sauternes/autumn plum and stawberry crumbles

FOOD PREP
Roast fennel and olive salad (x 2) is a great starter that you can prepare ahead of time. You can serve it cold or you can warm the vegetables in the oven. Jasmine rice pilaf with salt-roasted chicken (x 2) is easy to cook in a larger quantity. Serve the rice with steamed green or snake beans. For dessert, choose between the tamarillos or the plum and strawberry crumbles, which can both be made in advance.

LIQUID SUGGESTIONS
A full-bodied wooded chardonnay or a gutsy pinot noir would be great with the salad. A different combination or the same wines could be served with the main. With dessert, serve a late-harvest or a botrytis-affected resiling.

busy person's dinner for 6

mint couscous with fried tomatoes
sesame-crusted ocean trout
autumn plum and strawberry crumbles

FOOD PREP
For the starter, prepare the couscous beforehand without adding the mint. All you have to do when the guests arrive is fry the tomatoes and heat the couscous. For mains, the sesame-crusted ocean trout with greens not only looks great but has a wonderful blend of flavours. Finish with cheeses and fruit, or try the plum crumbles if you have time. Shop the day before and pick up the trout on the way home on the day of your dinner.

LIQUID SUGGESTIONS
A semillon or sauvignon blanc or blend of these would suit the lemony zing of the couscous. An aged chardonnay or semillon or light, peppery pinot noir would complement the complexity of the salmon. With dessert, try a liqueur muscat or tokay, or an aged port.

country dinner

basics

Having a small selection of good-quality equipment will make life in the kitchen a whole lot easier. There is no need to have every piece of cooking equipment as well as the kitchen sink or that is exactly where you will spend most of your time—at the kitchen sink. Remember, when purchasing kitchen equipment, the price often reflects the quality and durability of the utensil.

baking dishes and tins

Be wise and buy a quality baking dish first go. A good, solid baking dish with ample sides is a must. The same rule goes for cake tins. Cheap cake tins can warp, rust and buckle. Purchase a few cake tins and removable-base tart tins and dry them in a warm oven after cleaning.

knives

A basic set is all you need. Purchase knives with a reputable brand name, which have solid, riveted handles. One medium- and one large-sized cook's knife for chopping, one small paring knife and one serrated knife make a basic set. You could add to this with a cleaver, and a boning or filleting knife. The only other must-have is a steel to keep your knives sharp.

pots and saucepans

Invest in a set of pots and saucepans that will last you a good 20 years or so. Select a range of saucepans from small through medium to large. You may also wish to have a stockpot large enough to boil up a good quantity of stock or soup. Choose saucepans with heavy bases that contain a layer of copper or aluminium for good conduction of heat.

frypans

A small, usually non-stick, frypan for omelettes or pancakes and a large, heavy-based frypan will cover most tasks. I prefer to have at least one non-stick frypan so I can cook more delicate things easily.

conical sieves, colanders

A fine conical sieve is great for straining sauces or pasta. Use colanders for draining the contents of a pot or for washing greens.

frypans

pots and saucepans

knives

baking dishes and tins

conical sieve and colander

veal cutlets with fried quince

roast herb lamb with apples

veal cutlets with fried quince

2 tablespoons oil
2 tablespoons sage leaves
cracked black pepper
4 thick veal cutlets
2 tablespoons butter
1 quince, peeled, cored and sliced
1/2 cup (4 fl oz) water

Heat oil in a frypan over high heat. Add sage and pepper to pan and cook for 1 minute. Add cutlets to pan and cook for 1 minute on each side or until veal is golden and sealed. Place cutlets in a baking dish and pour over pan juices. Heat butter in a frypan over medium heat. Add quince slices to pan and cook for 2 minutes on each side. Add water to pan, cover and cook for 5 minutes or until water has been absorbed. Place quince slices in baking dish with cutlets.
Cover dish and bake in a preheated 180°C (350°F) oven for 10–15 minutes or until veal is cooked to your liking. Serve veal with fried quinces, and buttered and peppered broad (fava) beans. Serves 4.

roast herb lamb with apples

1 large leg lamb, tunnel boned with shank bone left in
8 sprigs thyme
3 red onions, halved
1 tablespoon oil
3 green cooking apples, halved
stuffing
1 tablespoon oil
2 onions, chopped
2 tablespoons oregano leaves
2 tablespoons thyme leaves
3 cups fresh breadcrumbs
3 tablespoons seeded mustard

To make stuffing, place oil in a frypan over medium heat. Add onions to pan and cook for 4 minutes or until they are golden. Add oregano and thyme to pan and cook for 1 minute. Combine onion mixture, breadcrumbs and mustard. Press stuffing into the tunnel of the lamb leg. Place thyme sprigs around the outside of the lamb and tie it with string to secure. Place lamb in a baking dish with red onions and brush onions with oil.
Bake lamb in a preheated 200°C (400°F) oven for 25 minutes. Add apples to dish and cook for a further 25 minutes or until lamb is cooked to your liking, and apples and onions are very soft. Slice lamb and serve with baked onions and apples. Serves 4.
Note: ask your butcher to tunnel bone the leg of lamb and leave the shank bone in.

roast garlic chicken with artichoke mash

2 heads garlic
1 tablespoon olive oil
4 single chicken breasts on the bone, skin removed
cracked black pepper
Jerusalem artichoke mash
750g (1 1/2 lb) Jerusalem artichokes
3 mashing potatoes, peeled and chopped
1/4 cup (2 fl oz) cream
2 tablespoons butter
cracked black pepper and sea salt

To prepare chicken, place unpeeled whole garlic heads in a baking dish and sprinkle with olive oil. Bake garlic in a preheated 200°C (400°F) oven for 20 minutes or until it is golden and soft. Remove garlic from dish and squeeze soft garlic cloves from their skins. Spread garlic over flesh of chicken and top with pepper. Place chicken in a baking dish, cover and bake in a preheated 150°C (300°F) oven for 30 minutes or until chicken is tender.
To make artichoke mash, place a saucepan of water over high heat and allow water to rapidly simmer. Peel artichokes and immediately drop them into simmering water, to stop discolouration. Add potatoes to pan. Simmer vegetables for 8–12 minutes or until they are tender, then drain.
Place cream and butter in a saucepan and heat until mixture is almost simmering. Pour hot cream mixture over drained vegatables and mash with salt and pepper until smooth. To serve, place mash on serving plates and top with roast chicken. Serve with steamed beans. Serves 4.

simple roast tomato soup

14 ripe tomatoes, halved
1 head garlic
2 brown onions
4 cups (32 fl oz) vegetable stock*
3 tablespoons chopped basil
2 tablespoons chopped mint
cracked black pepper and sea salt

Place tomatoes, garlic and onions on a baking tray.
Place tray in a preheated 160°C (315°F) oven and bake for 45 minutes or until tomatoes are very soft, and garlic and onions are golden.
Remove garlic and onions from their skins, and chop onion. In a saucepan, cook garlic and onions over medium heat for 3 minutes. Place onion mixture, tomatoes and half the stock in a food processor or blender, and process until mixture is roughly chopped.
Return soup to saucepan. Add remaining stock, basil, mint, and pepper and salt to taste. Allow soup to simmer for 5 minutes. Serves 4 to 6 as a starter.

roast garlic chicken with artichoke mash

simple roast tomato soup

soft polenta with red wine roast beef

braised pickled lamb shanks

soft polenta with red wine roast beef

600g (1 1/4 lb) piece Scotch or eye fillet
2 cups (16 fl oz) red wine
1 tablespoon cracked black pepper
3 tablespoons chopped rosemary
3 tablespoons chopped lemon thyme
1 tablespoon crushed juniper berries
soft polenta
1 litre (32 fl oz) hot water
2 cups (16 fl oz) milk
1 1/4 cups polenta
sea salt and pepper
85g (3 oz) butter
1/2 cup grated parmesan cheese

Trim beef of any fat or sinew. Place beef in a shallow dish with red wine and allow to marinate for 2 hours, turning once. Drain marinade and pat beef dry. Combine pepper, rosemary, thyme and juniper berries. Roll beef in herb mixture to coat. Place beef in a baking dish and bake in a preheated 150°C (300°F) oven for 45 minutes or until it is cooked to your liking.
To make polenta, place water and milk in a heavy-based saucepan over medium heat until liquid is simmering. Slowly pour polenta into water while whisking to combine. Reduce heat to as low as possible. Cover and cook polenta, stirring occasionally with a wooden spoon so polenta doesn't stick to base of pan, for 20–25 minutes. Stir through salt, pepper, butter and parmesan.
To serve, place polenta on serving plates. Slice beef and place slices on polenta. Serves 4.

roast vegetable risotto

750g (1 1/2 lb) sweet potato, peeled and chopped
5 Roma (egg) tomatoes
2 leeks, halved
2–3 tablespoons olive or herb oil
2 tablespoons lemon thyme leaves
cracked black pepper
risotto
4–4 1/2 cups (32–36 fl oz) vegetable* or chicken stock*
1 cup (8 fl oz) white wine
1 tablespoon oil
2 cups arborio* rice
1 tablespoon rosemary leaves
2 teaspoons grated lemon rind
1/2 cup grated parmesan cheese
cracked black pepper and sea salt

To cook vegetables, place sweet potato, tomatoes and leeks in a baking dish. Drizzle vegetables with olive oil and sprinkle with lemon thyme and pepper. Prick tomatoes with a fork, place vegetables in a preheated 200°C (400°F) oven and bake for 35 minutes or until they are golden and soft.
To make risotto, place stock and wine in a saucepan over medium heat and allow mixture to slowly simmer.
Heat oil in a large saucepan over medium heat. Add rice, rosemary and lemon rind, and cook for 3–4 minutes or until rice is transparent. Add a cup of stock mixture to rice and stir until liquid has been absorbed.
Continue adding stock, a cup at a time, and stirring until liquid has been absorbed. When all stock has been used, the rice should be soft and creamy. If the rice is a little hard, add some boiling water. Stir though parmesan, and pepper and salt to taste.
To serve, place risotto on serving plates and top with roast vegetables. Serve risotto with extra parmesan and pepper. Serves 4 to 6.

roast vegetable risotto

veal roasted on herbs with sugar-roasted parsnips

wheat and rye bread

veal roasted on herbs with sugar-roasted parsnips

2 heads garlic

olive oil

1 kg (2 lb) standing rib or veal rack

6 sprigs bay leaves

8 sprigs rosemary

8 sprigs oregano

2 cups (16 fl oz) white wine

sugar-roasted parsnips

750g (1½ lb) small parsnips, peeled

2 tablespoons oil

3 tablespoons brown sugar

2 tablespoons butter

Place garlic in a baking dish, sprinkle with a little oil and bake in a preheated 200°C (400°F) oven for 20 minutes or until garlic is golden and soft. Squeeze garlic cloves from skins and spread garlic over veal.

Place bay leaves, rosemary and oregano in a pile in a baking dish and pour wine over. Top herbs and wine with veal and bake at 200°C (400°F) for 35–45 minutes or until veal is cooked to your liking.

While veal is cooking, halve parsnips and place them in a baking dish with oil. Bake at 200°C (400°F) for 20 minutes, then sprinkle sugar over parsnips and dot them with butter. Cook for a further 10 minutes, shaking the baking dish to coat parsnips with sugar.

To serve, slice veal and serve with the sugar-roasted parsnips. Serves 4.

braised pickled lamb shanks

12 small pearl or small brown onions

3 cloves garlic, peeled

1 tablespoon juniper berries

2 teaspoons shredded lemon rind

8 pickled lamb shanks (see note below)

4 cups (32 fl oz) beef stock*

1 cup (8 fl oz) red wine

8 very small parsnips, peeled

4 Roma (egg) tomatoes, peeled

⅓ cup flat-leaf (Italian) parsley

Place onions, garlic, juniper berries, lemon rind, lamb shanks, stock, wine, parsnips and tomatoes in a large baking dish. Cover dish and bake in a preheated 180°C (350°F) oven for 45 minutes. Turn shanks, cover and bake for a further 30 minutes or until they are tender. Serve shanks in deep bowls with pan broth and lots of chopped flat-leaf (Italian) parsley. Serves 4.

Note: ask your butcher to put some lamb shanks in brine solution, or pickle, for 1–2 days.

wheat and rye bread

1½ cups (12 fl oz) warm water

2½ teaspoons active dry yeast

1 cup plain (all-purpose) flour

½ cup rye flour

½ cup wholemeal plain (all-purpose) flour

1 teaspoon active dry yeast, extra

1 cup (8 fl oz) warm water, extra

3½–4 cups plain (all-purpose) flour, extra

1 cup wholemeal plain (all-purpose) flour, extra

½ cup coarsely cracked wheat

1 tablespoon sea salt

Place water and yeast in a bowl and allow to stand until mixture has a foamy top. Combine plain, rye and wholemeal flours and mix into yeast mixture until smooth. Cover bowl with a damp tea towel and allow to stand for 1 hour or until mixture has doubled in size.

Place mixture in the bowl of an electric mixer fitted with a dough hook. Combine extra yeast and water, and allow to stand for 5 minutes. While the mixer's motor is running, add extra yeast mixture, extra plain and wholemeal flours, cracked wheat and salt to the bowl. Allow the dough hook to make the mixture into dough and then knead dough with the dough hook for a further 10 minutes.

Cover dough and allow it to prove* and double in size for about 1½–2 hours. Place dough on a lightly floured surface and knead lightly. Shape dough into a tight loaf and allow it to prove* for 1 hour.

To bake, preheat a baking stone or a few terracotta tiles in a 220°C (425°F) oven for 20 minutes. Fill a spray bottle with water and spray the oven walls to create steam, then shut the door quickly. Make a few slashes in the top of the bread and slide it onto the preheated stone or tiles. Spray oven walls with water again and shut the door quickly.

Reduce heat to 200°C (400°F) and bake bread for 1 hour or until the crust is a deep golden colour and the bread sounds hollow when tapped. Serve bread warm with the best quality butter you can find. Makes 1 large loaf.

Note: dough may appear to be tacky, but the wheat will absorb moisture during the proving* process.

baked quince with quince panna cotta

steamed persimmon pudding

baked quince with quince panna cotta

4 quinces, peeled and halved
3 cups sugar
6 cups (48 fl oz) boiling water
1 vanilla bean
quince panna cotta
2 cups (16 fl oz) cream
½ cup (4 fl oz) milk
3 teaspoons gelatine
¼ cup (2 fl oz) boiling water

Place quinces in a large baking dish. Combine sugar and water, and mix to dissolve sugar. Add sugar and water mixture and vanilla bean to baking dish, and cover. Bake quinces in a preheated 150°C (300°F) oven, turning them twice, for 4–5 hours or until they are a blushing pink colour and soft.
To make panna cotta, remove 1 cup (8 fl oz) of simmering liquid from quinces in baking dish and place in a saucepan. Bring liquid to the boil and simmer until ½ cup (4 fl oz) remains. Add cream and milk to liquid and allow to heat. Sprinkle gelatine over boiling water and stir to dissolve. Add gelatine mixture to cream mixture. Pour mixture into 8 small, greased ramekins and refrigerate for 4 hours or until panna cotta is set.
Before serving, heat quinces gently in remaining syrup in the oven and place them on serving plates. Unmould panna cotta onto serving plates and serve. Serves 8.

steamed persimmon pudding

1½ cups self-raising (self-rising) flour
½ teaspoon baking powder (baking soda)
60g butter, softened
2 eggs
⅔ cup sugar
3 tablespoons golden syrup
1½ cups persimmon purée

Place flour, baking powder, butter, eggs, sugar, golden syrup and persimmon purée into the bowl of an electric mixer and beat for 2–3 minutes or until mixture is well combined. Pour mixture into a greased pudding mould, cover with paper and aluminium foil and tie tightly with string, or cover with a tight-fitting lid.
Place pudding mould in a large saucepan of boiling water and allow the water to come three-quarters of the way up the sides of the pudding mould. Boil pudding for 2 hours or until it is cooked when tested with a skewer. Stand pudding for 5 minutes before inverting onto a serving plate and serving with persimmon slices and thick, honey-flavoured cream. Serves 8.

fig and brioche pudding

12 large slices brioche
5 figs, thickly sliced
2 cups (16 fl oz) cream
2 cups (16 fl oz) milk
3 eggs
⅓ cup sugar
1 teaspoon vanilla extract
demerara sugar

Alternately layer brioche and figs in a greased 5-cup capacity ovenproof dish. Place cream, milk, eggs, sugar and vanilla extract in a bowl and whisk to combine. Pour egg mixture over brioche and figs in dish and allow to stand for 5 minutes. Sprinkle top of brioche with demerara sugar and place dish in a baking dish. Fill baking dish with enough hot water to come halfway up the sides of the inner dish. Bake pudding in a preheated 180°C (350°F) oven for 25 minutes or until pudding is set. Serve pudding hot with scoops of vanilla bean ice cream. Serves 4 to 6.

lime curd tarts with pomegranate

1 quantity (350g or 12 oz) sweet shortcrust pastry*
1 pomegranate
lime curd
90g (3 oz) butter
¾ cup caster (superfine) sugar
½ cup (4 fl oz) lime juice
2 eggs, lightly beaten

Roll out pastry on a lightly floured surface until it is 2mm (⅛ inch) thick. Cut pastry into circles to fit twelve 6cm (2½ inch) tart tins. Prick pastry bases, line them with baking paper and fill with pastry weights or rice. Bake shells in a preheated 200°C (400°F) oven for 4 minutes. Remove paper and weights, and cook shells for a further 4 minutes or until they are golden.
To make lime curd, place butter, sugar, lime juice and eggs in a heatproof bowl over rapidly simmering water. Stir mixture until curd thickens, then cover and refrigerate until curd is cold.
To serve, remove pomegranate seeds from the shell. Spoon lime curd into tart shells and top with pomegranate seeds. Makes 12.

fig and brioche pudding

lime curd tarts with pomegranate

menu ideas

big family dinner for 8

simple roast tomato soup
wheat and rye bread
roast herb lamb with apples
steamed persimmon pudding

FOOD PREP
Make the simple roast tomato soup (x 2) up to 1 day
beforehand, heat and serve it with the wheat and rye bread
or buy some good-quality bread to accompany the soup. For
mains, 1 large or 2 small roast herb lamb with apples, with a
few extra onions and apples in the pan, will be enough to go
around. Place the roast in the oven before serving the soup.
Serve the lamb with some roasted root vegetables or
steamed beans and broccoli. Steamed persimmon pudding is
a warming and comforting dessert.

LIQUID SUGGESTIONS
Choose a well-flavoured pinot noir or a cabernet sauvignon
for the soup. Continue with a cabernet sauvignon with the
lamb or move on to a shiraz. Serve dessert with a sweet
sticky wine served at room temperature or just quickly chilled.
Or you could skip the sticky and have a coffee and a port.

winter dinner for 6

roast vegetable risotto
braised pickled lamb shanks
fig and brioche pudding

FOOD PREP
The risotto makes a good, hearty starter with the braised
pickled lamb shanks (x 1½) and a large bowl of steamed
greens to follow. The shanks can be made a day ahead and
reheated. To finish, small portions of fig and brioche pudding
will top things off nicely. Arrange brioche and figs in baking
dish ahead of time and pour over custard, which can also be
prepared ahead of time, just before baking.

LIQUID SUGGESTIONS
To start, a well-rounded cabernet sauvignon or merlot blend
makes a good accompaniment for the risotto. Move on to a
spicy shiraz with the shanks and a liqueur muscat with the
pudding.

cosy dinner for 2

simple roast tomato soup
veal roasted on herbs with sugar-roasted parsnips
baked quince with quince panna cotta

FOOD PREP
Serve the simple roast tomato soup with some warm bread
for starters. Freeze the leftover soup for a Sunday afternoon.
Follow the soup with the veal roasted on herbs with sugar-
roasted parsnips. The baked quince with quince panna cotta
will top off the evening well and can be made 1 day ahead of
time.

LIQUID SUGGESTIONS
The robust and well-flavoured soup would be good with a
rich pinot noir or with a cabernet sauvignon. Serve the same
wine with the main or change to a merlot blend with lots of
flavour. The dessert would suit a chilled late-harvest riesling.

sunday lunch for 4

soft polenta with red wine roast beef/roast garlic chicken with
artichoke mash
baked quince with quince panna cotta

FOOD PREP
Skip the starters or serve warm bread with a few pastes or
spreads. You could serve the soft polenta with red wine roast
beef or the roast garlic chicken with artichoke mash for mains
and then the baked quince with quince panna cotta, which
can be made well in advance, for dessert.

LIQUID SUGGESTIONS
Serve a light pinot when your guests arrive to get those
tastebuds ready for a well-flavoured, hearty lunch. Serve a
big-flavoured cabernet sauvignon or shiraz with the beef or, if
you choose the chicken, a grenache blend or a well-flavoured
pinot noir. Serve the quinces with a liqueur tokay or a smooth
and sticky dessert wine.

red carpet dining

basics

It's special-occasion time, so polish up your best glasses and clean the silver. Don't be afraid to pull out the family heirlooms. Formal dining occasions are becoming increasingly rare so, when you do roll out the red carpet, do it with simple style and as much finesse as possible. For a smooth performance, prepare as much of the food as you can ahead of time, set and dress the table, and have the drinks and pre-dinner morsels ready to serve when your guests arrive.

napkins and napery

Use large thick white napkins and napery, or go for rich colours to accessorise and add variety, colour and warmth to your table.

glasses

I think it is more important to have good-quality glasses than different glasses for every occasion. Red and white wine can be served from the same generous wine glass. It makes more sense to buy a larger set of one type of glass. Clear glasses from the table and rinse them before serving different wine in the same glass. Dessert wine, port, liqueur or shot glasses are also handy to have.

cutlery

Just like fashion, plain, classic, good-quality cutlery will serve you well. Cutlery should balance easily in the hand and be effortless to use.

crockery

White crockery is always a safe bet and makes food look appetising and fresh. Co-ordinate large serving ware in white or with colours to match.

table centre

A table centre can not only be beautiful but is also a great way to scent a room—whether it is a bowl of quinces or ruby grapefruit that give off their natural fragrance, or flowers.

cutlery

napkins

table centre

crockery

Please sit here

Your Place

glasses

potato galettes with soft quail eggs

oysters with cucumber salad

potato galettes with soft quail eggs

6 quail eggs
60g (2 oz) salmon roe
potato galettes
8 kipfler (finger) potatoes, peeled and thinly sliced
olive oil
1 cup grated parmesan cheese
cracked black pepper
1 leek, shredded

To make potato galettes, brush slices of potato with a little oil, and sprinkle with parmesan and pepper. Form 6 piles of potato slices and top piles with leeks. Place piles on a lined baking tray and bake in a preheated 200°C (400°F) oven for 20–25 minutes or until potatoes are golden and crisp.
To serve, place quail eggs in simmering water for 45 seconds to 1 minute, then peel. Place galettes on warm serving plates and top with a halved quail egg and salmon roe. Serves 6 as a starter.

oysters with cucumber salad

36 freshly shucked oysters
cucumber salad
1 Lebanese cucumber, shredded
¼ cup chervil* leaves
2 tablespoons lime juice
cracked black pepper

To make cucumber salad, combine cucumber, chervil, lime juice and pepper.
To serve, lift oyster from its shell and place a spoonful of cucumber salad on the shell. Top with oyster and serve. Serves 4 to 6 as a starter.

chicken roasted on tomatoes and eggplant

6 Roma (egg) tomatoes, halved
2 small eggplants (aubergines), halved and scored
olive oil
pepper
2 tablespoons oregano leaves
2 tablespoons butter
1 tablespoon lemon juice
4 chicken breast fillets, skin on

Place tomatoes and eggplants (aubergines) in a baking dish, drizzle with oil, and sprinkle with pepper and oregano leaves. Bake vegetables in a preheated 180°C (350°F) oven for 35 minutes or until they are soft.
Heat butter and lemon juice in a frypan over high heat. Add chicken to pan and cook, skin side down, for 3–4 minutes or until it is well browned. Place chicken on tomatoes and eggplants (aubergines) in oven and spoon over lemon butter. Reduce heat to 150°C (300°F) and bake for 15 minutes or until chicken is cooked through. Serve with pan juices. Serves 4.

crispy duck lasagne

8 small wonton wrappers
oil for deep frying
spiced duck
1 Chinese barbecue duck*
1 tablespoon oil
1 leek, shredded
120g (4 oz) fresh shiitake mushrooms*
2 teaspoons shredded orange rind
¼ cup (2 fl oz) Chinese cooking (shao hsing) wine

To prepare spiced duck, remove all the meat from the duck and slice, then set aside.
Heat oil in a frypan or wok over high heat. Add leek and cook for 6 minutes or until it is golden. Add mushrooms, orange rind and wine to pan and cook for 2 minutes. Add duck to pan and cook for 2 minutes or until it is heated through.
Cook wontons, a few at a time, in hot oil until they are golden and crisp, then drain on absorbent paper. Place a wonton on 4 individual serving plates. Top wonton with a spoonful of duck mixture. Top this with another wonton. Serve immediately. Serves 4 as a starter or serve with steamed greens as a main meal.

chicken roasted on tomatoes and eggplant

olive-crusted lamb with couscous salad

crisy duck lasagne

spiced tuna with udon and dashi

olive-crusted lamb with couscous salad

750g (1½ lb) lamb backstrap or eye of loin
½ cup green olives
2 teaspoons grated lemon rind
2 tablespoons chopped flat-leaf (Italian) parsley
2 tablespoons chopped mint
couscous salad
1½ cups couscous
1½ cups (12 fl oz) boiling vegetable stock*
2 tablespoons olive oil
2 onions, sliced
200g (6½ oz) green beans, trimmed
2 tablespoons chopped flat-leaf (Italian) parsley, extra
⅓ cup caper berries*
2 tablespoons lemon juice

Trim lamb of any fat or sinew. Finely chop olives and combine with lemon rind, parsley and mint. Spread seasoning over lamb and place lamb in an oiled baking dish. Place dish in a preheated 160°C (315°F) oven for 30 minutes or until lamb is cooked to your liking.
To make couscous salad, place couscous and stock in a bowl and set aside until the stock is absorbed. Heat oil in a frypan over high heat. Add onions and cook for 5 minutes or until they are golden. Add beans, extra parsley, caper berries and lemon juice to pan and cook for 4 minutes. Add couscous to pan and heat through.
To serve, place couscous on serving plates. Slice lamb thickly, place slices on top of couscous and serve with lemon wedges. Serves 4.

rosemary lamb cutlets with truffle oil mash

12 lamb cutlets
12 sprigs rosemary
1 tablespoon oil
1 tablespoon seeded mustard
truffle oil mash
8 mashing potatoes
50g (1¾ oz) butter
3 tablespoons cream
truffle infused oil

Trim cutlets and tie a sprig of rosemary around each cutlet. Combine oil and mustard, and brush over lamb.
To make the truffle oil mash, peel and chop potatoes. Place potatoes in a saucepan of boiling water and cook until they are soft, then drain. Place butter and cream in pan and cook until butter is melted and cream is hot. Add potatoes to pan and mash until smooth. Season mash with salt.
To cook lamb, preheat a frypan or grill over high heat. Add cutlets to pan and cook for 1–2 minutes on each side or until lamb is cooked to your liking.
To serve, place mash on serving plates and drizzle with truffle oil. Place cutlets on plate with mash. Serve with steamed asparagus. Serves 4.

rosemary lamb cutlets with truffle oil mash

slow-roasted spice crust salmon

squid ink pasta with salmon and roe

spiced tuna with udon and dashi

3 tablespoons mild chilli oil
2 tablespoons lime juice
2 tablespoons balsamic vinegar
1 tablespoon shredded ginger
1 tablespoon chopped coriander
4 tuna steaks
200g (6½ oz) udon noodles*
3 cups (24 fl oz) dashi broth*
2 shallots, sliced

Combine chilli oil, lime juice, balsamic vinegar, ginger and coriander. Add tuna to marinade and refrigerate for 2 hours, turning once.
To serve, heat udon noodles in boiling water, drain and place in bowls. Top noodles with hot dashi broth and shallots. Preheat a frypan or grill over high heat. Cook tuna for 30 seconds to 1 minute on each side or until it is well seared. Serve tuna on top of noodles and broth. Serves 4.

slow-roasted spice crust salmon

650g (1 lb 5 oz) salmon fillet, skin removed
2 tablespoons coriander seeds
cracked black pepper
3 tablespoons olive oil
1½ cups (12 fl oz) cream
1 kaffir lime* leaf
1 tablespoon coriander leaves
1 toasted nori* sheet, finely sliced
caviar for serving, optional

Remove any visible bones from salmon, and wash and pat dry. Toast coriander seeds in a frypan over medium heat for 3–5 minutes or until they are aromatic. Crush coriander seeds with a mortar and pestle, and spread over salmon. Cut salmon into 4 pieces and sprinkle lightly with pepper. Place oil in a baking dish and add salmon to dish. Bake in a preheated 120°C (250°F) oven for 20 minutes or until salmon has changed colour and is cooked medium.
While salmon is cooking, place cream, kaffir lime leaf and coriander leaves in a saucepan and allow to simmer. Simmer the sauce until it has reduced by at least half.
To serve, spoon a little of the sauce onto serving plates, top with a piece of salmon, sprinkle with nori slices and place a spoonful of caviar on the side. Serve with steamed greens. Serves 4 as a starter.

squid ink pasta with salmon and roe

500g (1 lb) fresh squid ink pasta
90g (3 oz) butter
3 tablespoons lime juice
2 tablespoons chervil* sprigs
400g (13 oz) salmon fillet, thickly sliced
cracked black pepper
100g (3¼ oz) salmon roe

Place pasta in a saucepan of boiling water for 5–6 minutes or until it is al dente, then drain. While pasta is cooking, place butter and lime juice in a frypan over high heat and cook until mixture is bubbling. Add chervil and salmon to pan and cook salmon for 30 seconds on each side or until it is well sealed.
Place pasta on warm serving plates and top with salmon, pan juices, pepper and salmon roe. Serve immediately. Serves 6 as a starter or 4 as main meal.

grilled scampi tails on lemon and chive risotto

8 green (raw) scampi (langoustine) or fresh-water yabbies
60g (2 oz) butter melted
1 tablespoon small sage leaves
cracked black pepper
lemon and chive risotto
4½ cups (36 fl oz) vegetable* or chicken stock*
1 cup (8 fl oz) dry white wine
2 tablespoons oil
2 teaspoons grated lemon rind
2 cups arborio rice*
3 tablespoons lemon juice
¼ cup snipped chives
½ cup grated parmesan cheese

To make lemon and chive risotto, place stock and wine in a saucepan over medium heat, and allow to slowly simmer. Place oil in a large saucepan over medium heat. Add lemon rind and rice to pan, and cook for 1 minute.
Add hot stock mixture to rice, a few cups at a time, stirring frequently so the rice doesn't stick and the risotto has a creamy texture. Continue adding stock until liquid has been absorbed and rice is tender. If the rice is not tender, add a little boiling water. Stir lemon juice, chives and parmesan through rice.
While the risotto is cooking, prepare the scampi (langoustine). Cut scampi (langoustine) tails in half, remove the claws and set aside. Place tails and claws on a baking tray, and sprinkle with butter, sage and pepper. Place tray under a hot preheated grill and cook for 2–3 minutes or until scampi (langoustine) are cooked. To serve, place risotto on plates and top with grilled scampi (langoustine). Serves 4.

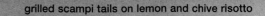

grilled scampi tails on lemon and chive risotto

caramelised vanilla risotto pudding

2 tablespoons butter
1 cup arborio rice*
1 vanilla bean, split
2 cups (16 fl oz) water
2 cups (16 fl oz) milk
3 tablespoons sugar
1 teaspoon vanilla extract
1 cup (8 fl oz) cream
2 egg yolks
extra sugar

Heat butter in a saucepan over moderate heat. Add rice to pan and cook for 3 minutes, then add vanilla bean.
Place water and milk in a saucepan over moderate heat and allow to simmer. Add milk mixture to rice 1 cup at a time, stirring occasionally, until liquid has been absorbed. Remove vanilla bean, and stir sugar and vanilla extract through rice. Whisk together cream and egg yolks, stir into risotto and cook until cream has been absorbed.
To serve, place risotto on serving plates and sprinkle with extra sugar. Heat a large metal cook's spoon or brûlée iron* over high heat. Run the spoon or iron over the sugar until it melts and is golden. Serve caramelised risotto with warm blood plums. Serves 4 to 6.

chocolate raspberry dessert cake

185g (6 oz) butter
185g (6 oz) dark chocolate, chopped
3 eggs
1/2 teaspoon vanilla extract
1 1/2 cups caster (superfine) sugar
1 cup plain (all-purpose) flour
2/3 cup self-raising (self-rising) flour
1/2 cup almond meal
1 cup raspberries

Place butter and chocolate in a saucepan over low heat and stir until melted, then cool slightly.
Place eggs, vanilla extract and sugar in a bowl and beat until mixture is light and thick. Fold through flours, almond meal, chocolate mixture and half the raspberries.
Pour mixture into a 20cm (8 inch) round cake tin lined with non-stick baking paper. Sprinkle over remaining raspberries and bake in a preheated 180°C (350°F) oven for 35 minutes or until top of cake is firm to touch. Cool cake before cutting, and serve with strong espresso, extra raspberries and thick cream. Serves 8 to 10.

caramelised vanilla risotto pudding

chocolate raspberry dessert cake

little lemon curd tarts

1 quantity (350g or 12 oz) sweet shortcrust pastry*
filling
¾ cup caster (superfine) sugar
3 eggs
¾ cup (6 fl oz) cream
½ cup (4 fl oz) lemon juice
1 teaspoon grated lemon rind

Roll out pastry on a lightly floured surface until it is 2mm
(⅛ inch) thick. Cut pastry into 6 cirlces to fit six 1-cup
(8 fl oz) capacity muffin tins. Prick pastry, line with non-stick
baking paper and fill with rice or baking weights. Bake
pastry in a preheated 200°C (400°F) oven for 5 minutes.
Remove rice or weights and paper, and bake pastry for a
further 4 minutes or until it is light golden.
To make filling, place sugar, eggs, cream, lemon juice and
rind in a bowl and mix to combine. Pour filling into tart
shells and bake in a 160°C (315°F) oven for 20 minutes or
until filling is just set. Cool tarts and serve with thick cream
and berries. Serves 6.

ice cream cones

vanilla bean ice cream
cones
¾ cup icing (confectioners) sugar
1 cup plain (all-purpose) flour
3 egg whites
90g (3 oz) butter, melted

To make cones, combine icing (confectioners) sugar, flour,
egg whites and butter, and allow to stand for 10 minutes.
Take 2 tablespoons of mixture and spread into a thin circle
on a baking tray lined with non-stick baking paper. Bake
wafers in a preheated 180°C (350°F) oven for 8–10 minutes
or until they are just beginning to brown on the edges.
Remove wafers from tray with a spatula and fold each one
around the end of a rolling pin to form a cone. Allow to
stand for 1 minute before removing cone from rolling pin.
To serve, fill cones with vanilla bean ice cream and store in
freezer or serve immediately. Serves 6 to 8.

little lemon curd tart

ice cream cone

menu ideas

'the in-laws are coming' dinner for 4

oysters with cucumber salad
slow-roasted spice crust salmon
olive-crusted lamb with couscous salad
chocolate raspberry dessert cake

FOOD PREP

It's make or break time so be sure to find out what they don't eat. A few oysters with cucumber salad, prepared ahead of time and refrigerated until they arrive, accompanied by a drink should settle everyone comfortably. Follow the oysters with the spice crust salmon and the lamb with couscous salad. For dessert, the chocolate raspberry dessert cake is fantastic and can be made 1 day in advance.

LIQUID SUGGESTIONS

Celebrate your guests' arrival with a dry sparkling white wine, which also goes well with the oysters. The salmon is best served with a lightly wooded chardonnay or semillon, then move to a spicy pinot noir or a full-bodied cabernet sauvignon. The dessert cake is perfect with a sweet glass of botrytis-affected riesling and a coffee. Don't forget to wrap extra cake for them to take home.

the boss's dinner for 6

oysters with cucumber salad
crispy duck lasagne
rosemary lamb cutlets with truffle oil mash
little lemon curd tarts

FOOD PREP

Serious red carpet time: don't be too showy or you may find yourself with a salary decrease. Simple and stylish is the way to go. Start with a few oysters with cucumber, prepared the day before and refrigerated until required, and then move on to the duck lasagne (x 1½). Serve mains of rosemary lamb cutlets with mash (x 1½) with a bowl of steamed baby spinach dressed with a squeeze of lemon and a sprinkling of black pepper and parmesan in the middle of the table. Prepare cutlets and potatoes beforehand and cook when required. Finish with lemon tarts, which can be made the morning before, and coffee and chocolate truffles. Perfect.

LIQUID SUGGESTIONS

Remember not to drink too much (slurring and boisterous behaviour in front of the boss is not a good look). Serve a dry sparkling white to toast your guests' arrival and to accompany the oysters. The duck lasagne is great with a sparkling red (that will surprise them) or a good pinot noir. The rosemary lamb is very full flavoured, so an aged cabernet sauvignon or shiraz is best. The lemon tarts have a zesty tang and are best served with a not-so-sweet sticky such as a late-harvest semillon. Finish in the lounge room with coffee, truffles and port.

formal dinner for 8

potato galettes with soft quail eggs
grilled scampi tails on lemon and chive risotto
chicken roasted on tomatoes and eggplant
ice cream cones

FOOD PREP

Seriously consider whether you really want to have more than 8 people for a formal dinner as glasses, crockery, cutlery and oven space often run short. As an appetiser, the potato galettes with soft quail eggs (x 2) are very impressive. Follow this with small serves of the grilled scampi on lemon and chive risotto and, for mains, the chicken roasted on tomatoes and eggplant (aubergine) (x 2) is quite easy to cook for 8 people. Dessert of ice cream cones filled with vanilla bean ice cream, which can be made ahead of time and stored in the freezer, is not only cute but simple.

LIQUID SUGGESTIONS

Serve sparkling dry white wine when your guests arrive followed by an aged semillon with the potato galettes. Move on to a sauvignon blanc with the risotto and an aged, lightly wooded chardonnay or a pinot noir with the chicken. Serve the ice cream cones with a liqueur tokay and then coffee with cognac or port.

10

tea party

basics

Tea is an evergreen shrub that grows in mountainous, subtropical to tropical areas. There are thousands of types of tea and the differences are based on where the tea is grown, how it is plucked and how it is processed.

black tea

These teas are fully fermented and black in appearance. Varieties of black tea include darjeeling, assam, ceylon and keemun. When black teas are brewed they have a rich amber colour. During processing, some black teas are smoked for extra flavour.

oolong

Oolong tea is partially fermented—a cross between green tea and black tea. It should have large, rusty brown leaves with silver tips. The tea is fragrant with a distinctive sweet aftertaste.

green tea

Green tea has been made by the Chinese and Japanese for centuries. Green tea is not fermented; it is made by sun-drying the tender tea leaves and then either pan firing them in a special wok or lightly steaming them. Steaming the tea leaves takes away the bitter flavour. The tea leaves should be light green and have a delicate, subtle taste. Some varieties of green tea are gunpowder, lung ching, sencha and gen mai cha.

herbal teas

Herbal teas are not really tea but they are growing in popularity. They may be fermented teas combined with the dried fruits, flowers, leaves, roots or stems of plants, or they may be dried herbal combinations. These teas are brewed in the same way as regular tea and are sometimes used as naturopathic remedies. Popular herbal teas include lemongrass, chamomile, peppermint and raspberry.

white tea

White tea is a rare tea found in China. The leaves are not fermented. It is used for special occasions, such as weddings, and is rather expensive. The silver tips stand on end when they are served. Only a few leaves are needed to make a cup of tea.

oolong tea

green tea

white tea or buddha's tears

herbal tea

black tea

little chocolate mud cakes

baby raspberry and coconut cake

mint, lemon and ginger iced tea & banana and palm sugar wontons

candied lemon and lime tart

little chocolate mud cakes

300g (10 oz) dark chocolate, chopped
300g (10 oz) butter
5 eggs
1/2 cup sugar
3/4 cup self-raising (self-rising) flour, sifted

Place chocolate and butter in a saucepan over low heat and stir until smooth, then set aside.
Place eggs and sugar in a bowl, and beat until light and fluffy (about 6 minutes). Fold egg mixture through flour and chocolate mixture. Pour mixture into 12 paper-lined or well-greased patty tins and bake in a preheated 160°C (315°F) oven for 25 minutes or until cakes feel firm to touch. Serve cakes warm with a sprinkling of good-quality cocoa.
Makes 12.
Note: this cake can also be cooked in a base-lined and greased 23cm (9 inch) round cake tin. Bake at 160°C (315°F) for 45 minutes or until cake feels firm to touch.

baby raspberry and coconut cakes

125g (4 oz) unsalted butter
1/4 cup almond meal
3/4 cup desiccated coconut
1 2/3 cups icing (confectioners) sugar, sifted
1/2 cup plain (all-purpose) flour, sifted
1/2 teaspoon baking powder (baking soda)
5 egg whites
2/3 cup raspberries, fresh or frozen

Place butter in a saucepan over low heat and cook until it is a very light golden colour. Place almond meal, coconut, icing (confectioners) sugar, flour and baking powder in a bowl and mix to combine. Add egg whites to bowl and mix. Add melted butter to bowl and continue to mix until combined.
Pour mixture into greased small brioche or patty tins. Sprinkle raspberries over the tops of the cakes. Preheat oven to 180°C (350°F) and bake for 12–15 minutes or until cakes are golden, springy to touch and moist in the centre. Serve with clotted cream and fruit tea. Makes 10.

mint, lemon and ginger iced tea

4 tablespoons peppermint tea leaves
8–10 slices ginger
1/2 cup mint leaves
2/3 cup sugar
6 cups (40 fl oz) water
1 cup (8 fl oz) lemon juice
extra ginger slices and mint leaves

Place tea, ginger, mint and sugar in a bowl. In a saucepan, bring water to the boil. Pour boiling water over mixture in bowl and allow to steep for 8 minutes, then strain. Stir lemon juice through tea and refrigerate for 2 hours or until tea is well chilled. Pour tea into a chilled jug and add extra ginger slices and mint leaves. Serve over ice. Makes 6 cups.
Note: this tea is a great body cleanser and pick-me-up.

banana and palm sugar wontons

2 bananas, thickly sliced
2 tablespoons lime juice
1/2 cup crumbled palm sugar
20 wonton wrappers
1 tablespoon cornflour (cornstarch)
2 tablespoons water
oil for shallow frying
icing (confectioners) sugar and cinnamon

Brush bananas lightly with lime juice and toss them in palm sugar. Place a piece of banana on one half of the wonton wrappers. Brush wonton edges with combined cornflour (cornstarch) and water, fold wonton wrappers to enclose and squeeze edges to seal.
Heat oil in a frypan until hot. Fry wontons for 1–2 minutes on each side or until they are golden. Drain wontons on absorbent paper. When wontons are cool enough to touch, toss them in icing (confectioners) sugar and cinnamon to coat. Serve warm with tea. Makes 20.

wild raspberry and lime tea & nectarine and basil iced tea

candied lemon and lime tarts

1 quantity (350g 12 oz) sweet shortcrust pastry*
filling
2 eggs, lightly beaten
2/3 cup (5 1/2 fl oz) lemon juice
1/3 cup (2 3/4 fl oz) lime juice
1 cup caster (superfine) sugar
2 cups (16 fl oz) cream
topping
2 cups sugar
1 cup (8 fl oz) water
2 lemons, sliced
3 limes, sliced

Roll out pastry on a lightly floured surface until it is 3mm (1/8 inch) thick. Cut pastry to fit eight 10cm (4 inch) deep tart tins. Prick pastry shells with a fork and line each with paper. Fill shells with rice or baking weights and bake in a preheated 200°C (400°F) oven for 5 minutes. Remove weights or rice and paper, and return shells to oven for 5 minutes or until pastry is light golden.
To make topping, place sugar and water in a large saucepan over low heat and stir gently until sugar has dissolved. Simmer the sugar syrup for 1 minute. Add lemon and lime slices to the pan in one layer. Cook over very low heat for 20 minutes or until rinds are soft. Do not boil. Place slices on non-stick baking paper, and allow them to cool and set.
To make filling, combine eggs, lemon and lime juice, sugar and cream. Pour mixture into pastry shells and bake at 160°C (315°F) for 10 minutes or until filling is beginning to set. Top tarts with slices of candied lemon and lime, and return to the oven. Bake for a further 10 minutes or until filling is just set. Makes 8.

wild raspberry and lime tea

5 tablespoons wild raspberry tea leaves
4 1/2 cups (36 fl oz) boiling water
1/2 cup sugar
1/3 cup (2 3/4 fl oz) lime juice
1 tablespoon shredded lime rind
1/2 cup raspberries

Place tea in water and allow to steep for 5 minutes. Strain and mix tea with sugar, lime juice and lime rind. Before serving, add raspberries to tea and serve over crushed ice. Makes 4 cups.

nectarine and basil iced tea

2 tablespoons darjeeling tea leaves
1 cup basil leaves
2 tablespoons mint leaves
1/2 cup sugar
5 cups (40 fl oz) water
4 large nectarines, puréed and sieved

Place tea, basil, mint and sugar in a bowl. In a saucepan, bring water to the boil. Pour boiling water over mixture in bowl and allow to steep for 6–7 minutes, then strain. Stir through puréed nectarine and refrigerate for 2 hours or until tea is well chilled. Pour tea into a jug with extra nectarine slices and basil leaves, and serve in tall glasses over ice. Serves 6.

ricotta, spinach and parmesan tarts

500g (1 lb) fresh ricotta
1/3 cup sour cream
1 egg, lightly beaten
cracked black pepper
pinch freshly grated nutmeg
500g (1 lb) baby English spinach leaves
1/2 cup finely grated parmesan cheese
1/4 cup chopped toasted pine nuts
1 tablespoon chopped dill

Place ricotta in a food processor and process until smooth. In a bowl, combine ricotta with sour cream, egg, pepper and nutmeg. Place spinach in a saucepan of boiling water for 5 seconds, then drain and chop. Squeeze any excess liquid from spinach.
Stir spinach, parmesan, pine nuts and dill into ricotta mixture. Spoon mixture into greased deep patty tins and bake at 160°C (315°F) for 25–30 minutes or until tarts are firm and golden. Makes 12.

ricotta, spinach and parmesan tarts

vanilla liquorice tea

green apple and vanilla tea sorbet

winter liquorice tea

5½ cups (44 fl oz) water
3 tablespoons liquorice root tea leaves
1 tablespoon orange rind strips with white pith
3 tablespoons mint leaves
½ cup (4 fl oz) orange juice
1–2 tablespoons honey

In a saucepan, bring water to the boil. Remove pan from heat and add tea, orange rind and mint leaves. Allow to steep for 5 minutes. Strain tea and return to pan. Bring tea to the boil, and add orange juice and honey to taste. Serve in warmed glasses. Serves 4.

green apple and vanilla tea sorbet

1 cup (8 fl oz) boiling water
3 tablespoons vanilla tea leaves
4 cups (32 fl oz) fresh green apple juice
2 teaspoons finely grated lemon rind
1 cup sugar

Place water and tea in a bowl and allow to steep for 5 minutes. Strain tea through a fine sieve and place in a saucepan with 1 cup (8 fl oz) of the apple juice. Add lemon rind and sugar to pan and stir over low heat until sugar has dissolved. Add remaining apple juice to mixture and refrigerate until cold.
Place mixture in an ice-cream maker and follow manufacturer's instructions until sorbet is frozen and scoopable. Alternatively, place mixture in a metal container and freeze for 1 hour, then whisk and freeze for another hour. Whisk and repeat. Serves 4 to 6.

apple honey tea cakes

1 tablespoon lemon juice
4 tablespoons demerara sugar
2 tablespoons butter
3 green apples, peeled and sliced
cake
185g (6 oz) butter
⅔ cup sugar
2 tablespoons honey
1 teaspoon vanilla extract
3 eggs
1½ cups plain (all-purpose) flour, sifted
1 teaspoon baking powder (baking soda)

Place lemon juice, sugar and butter in a frypan over high heat. Stir until mixture turns into a syrup. Add apples to pan, a few at a time, and cook for 1 minute on each side or until they are lightly browned, then set aside.
To make cake, place butter, sugar and honey in a bowl and beat until light and creamy. Add vanilla and eggs, one at a time, and beat well. Sift together flour and baking powder, and fold into butter mixture.
Layer the apple slices onto the bases of 8 well-greased or based-lined small rectangular 10cm x 5½ cm (4 x 2¼ inch) cake tins. Top apple with cake mixture until tins are three-quarters full. Bake at 160°C (315°F) for 25 minutes or until cakes are cooked when tested with a skewer. Invert cakes onto serving plates, and serve warm with cream and a pot of hot tea. Makes 8.

tea-soaked little pears

12 small corella* or cocktail pears
1 tablespoon lemongrass* tea leaves
3 tablespoons sugar
1 tablespoon mint leaves
2 cups (16 fl oz) boiling water
2 teaspoons lemon juice

Peel pears and set aside. Place lemongrass, sugar, mint and water in a jug and allow to infuse for 4 minutes, then strain. Place tea in a saucepan and heat until boiling. Place pears in the hot tea and allow to simmer for 8–10 minutes or until they are soft. Serve pears warm or chilled in bowls with the tea. Serves 4 to 6.

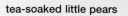

tea-soaked little pears

apple honey tea cakes

menu ideas

summer garden tea party for 10

baby raspberry and coconut cakes
little chocolate mud cakes
apple honey tea cakes
ricotta, spinach and parmesan tarts
nectarine and basil iced tea

FOOD PREP
A selection of small cakes and morsels allows guests to graze for the afternoon. Baby raspberry and coconut cakes, and little chocolate mud cakes can be prepared the day before and stored in airtight containers. Make apple honey tea cakes a few hours before serving. For a savoury touch, serve the ricotta, spinach and parmesan tarts, which can be made 1 day in advance and stored in the refrigerator until required.

LIQUID SUGGESTIONS
Serve a well-chilled fruit tea such as the nectarine and basil iced tea as well as a selection of teas and herbal teas. It is easier for each guest to have their own tea infuser, so they can choose their tea, and serve flasks of hot water. If you are serving iced fruit teas or hot herbal fruit teas, sparkling white wine is often a good accompaniment.

tea for 2

banana and palm sugar wontons
winter liquorice tea

FOOD PREP
A cosy tea for 2 on a cold afternoon would be great with warm banana and palm sugar wontons and winter liquorice tea. Prepare and cook wontons just before serving to ensure they are crisp.

LIQUID SUGGESTIONS
Share a pot of tea or serve the winter liquorice tea with shots of ouzo or pastis for extra warmth.

shower tea for 20

tea-soaked little pears
candied lemon and lime tarts
little chocolate mud cakes
ricotta, spinach and parmesan tarts

FOOD PREP
Set up a large table where people can serve themselves. A large bowl full of tea-soaked little pears (x 2), and plates of candied lemon and lime tarts (x 2), little chocolate mud cakes (x 2) and ricotta, spinach and parmesan tarts (x 2) will fill the table nicely. All of these recipes can be made 1 day in advance and stored in airtight containers in the refrigerator.

LIQUID SUGGESTIONS
Serve one or two different iced teas and a selection of hot teas as well as sparkling white wine and a fresh, slightly fruity riesling or an aged semillon.

afternoon tea for 6

tea-soaked little pears/baby raspberry and coconut cakes
green apple and vanilla tea sorbet/apple honey tea cakes
wild raspberry and lime tea

FOOD PREP
On a warm summer day, you could serve the tea-soaked little pears with the green apple and vanilla tea sorbet, which can both be made 1 day in advance. On a cooler day, try warm baby raspberry and coconut cakes or warm apple honey tea cakes.

LIQUID SUGGESTIONS
On a warm day, serve the wild raspberry and lime tea (be sure to use good-quality wild raspberry tea). On a cooler day, serve hot teas such as lemon and ginger or a lightly smoked black tea.

glossary

arborio rice

Taking its name from a village in the Piedmont region of northern Italy, this short-grain rice is used for risotto. It releases some of its starch when cooked, making a creamy savoury rice dish. Other varieties used for risotto include violone and carnaroli.

beef stock

1½ kg (3 lb) beef bones, cut into pieces
2 onions, quartered
2 carrots, quartered
2 stalks celery, cut into large pieces
assorted fresh herbs
2 bay leaves
10 peppercorns
4 litres (16 cups or 128 fl oz) water

Place bones in a baking dish and bake in a preheated 220°C (425°F) oven for 30 minutes. Add onions and carrots to dish and bake for a further 20 minutes. Remove bones, onions and carrots from dish and place in a stock pot or large saucepan. Skim fat from the top of juices in dish, then add 2 cups (8 fl oz) boiling water to dish to remove all the juices from the dish. Pour juices into saucepan.
Add celery, herbs, bay leaves, peppercorns and water to saucepan and bring to the boil. Allow mixture to simmer for 4–5 hours or until the stock has a good flavour. Skim top of stock during the cooking time. Strain stock and use as recipe requires. Refrigerate stock for up to 3 days or freeze for up to 3 months. Makes 2½–3 litres (10–12 cups or 80–96 fl oz).

betel leaves

Often called wild betel leaves or *cha plu*. The leaves are sold in bunches still on their stems. Remove leaves from stems and soak in cold water to refresh before using as wrappers for small morsels of food or shredded in salads. Available from Asian food stores.

black sesame seeds

From the same family as white sesame seeds, only black. Substitute white sesame seeds.

bonito flakes

Fine shavings from a dried bonito fish fillet. They look like rose-coloured wood shavings and are used for making dashi,* a stock used extensively in Japanese cooking. Available from Japanese or Asian supermarkets.

brûlée iron

A thick, heavy disk of steel on a long handle. It is heated over gas or eletric heat until very hot and then, in a sweeping motion, placed over the sugar on top of a crème brûlée to form a caramelised crust of sugar. The brûlée iron caramelises the sugar very quickly so the crème does not melt. Avaliable from cooks' shops. If you cannot find a brûlée iron, a small blowtorch from the hardware store will do the trick.

caper berries

The flower of the caper bush becomes an oval berry or fruit which is full of tiny seeds. Caper berries are sold with tender stems attached in vinegar or a brine solution. Available from good delicatessens.

chervil

A delicate, lacey-looking herb with a faint, sweet aniseed flavour. Its flavour diminishes after being chopped, so add to food just before serving.

chicken stock

1½ kg (3 lb) chicken bones, cut into pieces
2 onions, quartered
2 carrots, quartered
2 stalks celery, cut into large pieces
assorted fresh herbs
2 bay leaves
10 peppercorns
4 litres (16 cups or 128 fl oz) water

Place all ingredients in a stock pot or large saucepan and simmer for 3–4 hours or until stock is well flavoured. Skim fat from top of stock during the cooking time. Strain stock and use as recipe requires. Refrigerate stock for up to 3 days or freeze for up to 3 months. Makes 2½–3 litres (10–12 cups or 80–96 fl oz).

chinese barbecue duck

A cooked duck, spiced and barbecued in the traditional Chinese style. Avaliable from Chinese barbecue shops or from Chinese food stores.

chinese barbecue pork

Cooked pork meat, spiced and barbecued in the traditional Chinese barbecue style. Avaliable from Chinese barbecue shops or from Chinese food stores.

corella pears

Also known as cocktail pears, these small sweet pears are great for eating or poaching.

dariole moulds

Small cylindrical metal moulds, with slightly sloping sides, used to make puddings or set mousse in.

dashi broth

4 cups (32 fl oz) cold water
5cm (2 inch) piece kombu (dried
giant seaweed)
3 tablespoons dried bonito flakes*

Place water and kombu in a saucepan and heat until almost boiling. Before the water boils, remove kombu. If the water boils with the kombu in it, the dashi will have a bad odour. The kombu should be soft when removed, which indicates enough flavour has been released.
Place bonito flakes in the saucepan and bring to the boil. As soon as the water boils, remove pan from heat and allow to stand for 5 minutes before straining. The dashi is now ready to use as recipe requires.

fish stock

1 tablespoon butter
1 onion, finely chopped
750g (1½ lb) fish bones, chopped
1 cup (8 fl oz) white wine
1 litre (32 fl oz) water
10 peppercorns
3–4 sprigs mild herbs
1 bay leaf

Place butter and onion in a large saucepan over low heat and cook for 10 minutes or until onion is soft but not browned. Add fish bones, wine, water, peppercorns, herbs and bay leaf and simmer for 20 minutes. Skim the top of the stock while simmering, then strain and allow to cool. Use stock as recipe requires. Refrigerate stock for up to 2 days or freeze for 2 months. Makes 3–3½ cups (24–28 fl oz).
Note: do not simmer stock for more than 20 minutes or it sours.

framboise
Raspberry-flavoured brandy.

galangal
Looks similar to ginger with a pink tinge and can be purchased fresh, or sliced and bottled in brine.

glutinous rice
Predominantly used in sweets, glutinous rice is made up of plump, opaque grains of either white, black, short- or long-grain rice. The grains become sticky and sweet when cooked. Soak glutinous rice overnight before using if you are steaming it, or use it unsoaked if you are cooking it by absorption method. Available from Asian supermarkets.

green tea soba noodles
A speciality from northern Japan, these fine noodles are made from wheat flour and flavoured with green tea. Avaliable from Japanese and Asian supermarkets.

haloumi
Firm, salty white cheese made from sheep's milk. It has a stringy texture and is usually sold in brine. Available from delicatessens and some supermarkets.

hoi sin sauce
A thick, sweet-tasting Chinese sauce made from fermented soy beans, sugar, salt and red rice. Use it as a dipping or glazing sauce. Available from Asian food stores and supermarkets.

kaffir lime
The fragrant leaves are crushed or shredded and used in cooking, and the limes are used for their juice and rind mainly in Thai cuisine. Both the limes (fresh) and the leaves (available in packets, fresh or dried) are available from Asian grocers.

lemongrass
A tall lemon-scented grass used in Asian, mainly Thai cooking. Peel away outer leaves and use the tender root-end of the grass.

mascarpone
An Italian triple-cream curd-style fresh cheese, which has a similar consistency to double or thick cream. Available from good delicatessens and some supermarkets.

miso
A thick paste made from fermented and processed soy beans. Red miso is a combination of barley and soy beans and yellow miso is a combination of rice and soy beans.

non-reactive bowl
A ceramic or glass bowl, often necessary when high concentrations of vinegar or acid foods are used.

non-reactive saucepan
Often necessary when high concentrations of vinegar or acid foods are used. Use any saucepan except a saucepan made from aluminium.

nori
Thin sheets of dried and often toasted seaweed. Nori is used to wrap sushi and it is also added to Japanese soups. If you purchase untoasted nori, toast nori sheets over a low flame for 3 seconds on each side before using. Available in packets of sheets from Asian supermarkets.

proving

Process when a yeast mixture or dough is left covered in a warm, draught-free place to rise or prove.

rice paper rounds

Fine transparent circles made from a paste of rice and water. Before using, brush or dip in water until they are pliable. Available from Asian supermarkets.

shiitake mushrooms

Originally from Japan and Korea, these mushrooms have a distinctive woody and almost meaty flavour. They have brownish tops with a creamy underside. Available from good fruit and vegetable stores.

shortcrust pastry

2 cups plain (all-purpose) flour
155g (5 oz) butter, chopped
iced water

Place flour and butter in a food processor and process until mixture has formed fine crumbs. Add enough iced water to form a soft dough. Remove dough from food processor and knead lightly. Wrap dough in plastic wrap and refrigerate for 30 minutes before rolling to prevent shrinkage when baked.
Makes 1 quantity.

sterilised jar

Before putting foods into jars to be sealed and stored, the jars need to be sterilised. Sterilise jars by thoroughly washing jars in hot water. Place them on a baking tray, place tray in a preheated 100°C (200°F) oven and allow to heat for 30 minutes. Remove jars from oven, fill and seal.

sushi rice

1½ cups short-grain rice
2 cups (16 fl oz) water
5cm (2 inch) piece kombu (dried giant seaweed)
⅓ cup (2¾ fl oz) rice vinegar
2 teaspoons sugar
salt

Place rice in a colander and wash well under running water. Place rice in a saucepan with the water and place kombu on top of the rice. Cover and cook over medium heat. Remove kombu when water boils. Continue cooking, covered, and boiling for 2 minutes. Reduce heat to low and cook, covered, for 15 minutes or until all liquid has been absorbed. Place rice in a glass or ceramic bowl and toss with a wooden spoon or paddle until warm. Combine vinegar with sugar and salt. While tossing rice, sprinkle over vinegar mixture. Continue tossing rice until it has cooled. Cover with a damp cloth until ready to use.
Makes 1 quantity.
Note: when cooking rice, be sure to use a tight-fitting lid on the saucepan.

sweet flaky pastry

2 cups plain (all-purpose) flour
2 tablespoons caster (superfine) sugar
60g (2 oz) butter
150ml (5 fl oz) water
125g (4 oz) butter, extra, chopped

Place flour, sugar and butter in a food processor and process until mixture has formed fine crumbs. While motor is running, add water and process until mixture is a smooth dough. Roll dough on a lightly floured surface until it is 45cm (18 inches) long and 2cm (¾ inch) thick.

Soften extra chopped butter until it is pliable but not melted. Spread butter over two-thirds of the pastry. Take the pastry with no butter and fold it over one-third of the pastry. Fold pastry over again to encase butter. Press edges to seal. Cover and refrigerate for 15 minutes before rolling to use. Makes 1 quantity.

sweet shortcrust pastry

2 cups plain (all-purpose) flour
3 tablespoons caster (superfine) sugar
155g (5 oz) butter, chopped
iced water

Place flour, sugar and butter in a food processor and process until mixture has formed fine crumbs. Add enough iced water to form a soft dough. Remove dough from food processor and knead lightly. Wrap dough in plastic wrap and refrigerate for 30 minutes before rolling to prevent dough shrinking when baked. Makes 1 quantity.

szechwan peppercorns

Not really peppercorns at all, these are small, red-brown dried berries, native to the Chinese province of Szechwan. They have a very distinctive fragrance and flavour. Roast or heat them before crushing. Avaliable from Asian supermarkets.

tahini

A thick, smooth paste made from lightly toasted and ground sesame seeds. Available in jars from supermarkets.

udon noodles

White Japanese wheat noodles, which can be purchased fresh (in the refrigerator section) or dried. They come in a variety of thicknesses and lengths. Available from Japanese or Asian supermarkets.

vanilla beans

The fermented and dried seed pods of an orchid native to Mexico. They are long and dark, and good-quality beans are flexible and fragrant. Available from quality food stores and some supermarkets.

vegetable stock

4 litres (16 cups or 128 fl oz) water
1 parsnip
2 onions, quartered
1 clove garlic, peeled
2 carrots, quartered
300g (10 oz) roughly chopped cabbage
3 stalks celery, cut into large pieces
small bunch mixed fresh herbs
2 bay leaves
1 tablespoon peppercorns

Place all ingredients in a saucepan or stock pot and allow to simmer for 2 hours or until stock has a good flavour. Skim top of stock as it is simmering. Strain stock and use as recipe requires. Refrigerate stock for up to 4 days or freeze for up to 8 months. Makes 2½–3 litres (10–12 cups or 80–96 fl oz).

wasabi

A knobbly green root of the Japanese plant wasabia japonica. Wasabi has the same warming or stinging nasal sensation as horseradish, and is used with sushi and sashimi. Available in paste or powdered form from Asian grocers.

cup conversions

1 cup almonds, whole = 155g (5 oz)
1 cup baby English spinach leaves = 60g (2 oz)
1 cup basil leaves, whole, firmly packed = 50g (1¾ oz)
1 cup berries, mixed, chopped = 220g (7 oz)
1 cup cheese, parmesan, finely grated = 100g (3¼ oz)
1 cup coconut cream = 250g (8 oz)
1 cup coconut, desiccated = 90g (3 oz)
1 cup coriander leaves, whole = 30g (1 oz)
1 cup couscous = 185g (6 oz)
1 cup flour, plain (all-purpose) and self-raising (self-rising) = 125g (4 oz)
1 cup flour, wholemeal = 150g (5 oz)
1 cup honey = 350g (11¼ oz)
1 cup olives, medium green, unpitted = 175g (5¾ oz)
1 cup parsely, flat-leaf (Italian), whole = 20g (¾ oz)
1 cup polenta = 150g (5 oz)
1 cup raspberries, whole = 125g (4 oz)
1 cup rice, arborio, uncooked = 220g (7 oz)
1 cup rocket (arugula) leaves, roughly chopped = 45g (1½ oz)
1 cup sour cream = 250g (8 oz)
1 cup sugar, caster (superfine) = 250g (8 oz)
1 cup sugar, demerara = 220g (7 oz)
1 cup yoghurt, plain = 250g (8 oz)

inspirational books

Charmaine Solomon
Charmaine Solomon's encyclopedia of Asian food
William Heinemann, 1996

Max Allen
Red and white: wine made simple
Hamlyn, 1997

Allan Campion and Michele Curtis
Chilli jam: choosing and using Asian ingredients
Allen & Unwin, 1997

Stephanie Alexander
The cook's companion
Viking, 1996

index

Index compiled by Russell Brooks